DATE DUE			
Fac			
DEC 1 '80			
JAN 4 '84			
MAY 31 '84			
JAN 1 0 2003			

A HANDBOOK OF NON-VERBAL
GROUP EXERCISES

A HANDBOOK OF NON-VERBAL GROUP EXERCISES

By

KENNETH T. MORRIS, PH.D.

Associate Professor and Certified Consulting Psychologist
Counseling Center—Central Michigan University
Mount Pleasant, Michigan

and

KENNETH M. CINNAMON, M.A.

With a Foreword by

Goodwin Watson

Professor Emeritus, Columbia University and Core Faculty,
Union Graduate School

CHARLES C THOMAS • PUBLISHER
Springfield • Illinois • U.S.A.

Published and Distributed Throughout the World by

CHARLES C THOMAS • PUBLISHER

BANNERSTONE HOUSE

301-327 East Lawrence Avenue, Springfield, Illinois, U.S.A.

© *1975 by* CHARLES C THOMAS • PUBLISHER

ISBN 0-398-03228-9 (cloth)

ISBN 0-398-03239-4 (paper)

Library of Congress Catalog Card Number: 74-12328

With THOMAS BOOKS *careful attention is given to all details of manufacturing and design. It is the Publisher's desire to present books that are satisfactory as to their physical qualities and artistic possibilities and appropriate for their particular use.* THOMAS BOOKS *will be true to those laws of quality that assure a good name and good will.*

Printed in the United States of America

N-1

Library of Congress Cataloging in Publication Data

Morris, Kenneth T.
    A handbook of non-verbal group exercises.

    1. Group relations training. I. Cinnamon, Kenneth M. joint author. II. Title. [DNLM: 1. Group processes. 2. Nonverbal communication. 3. Sensitivity training. groups. HM134 M876h.]
HM134.M66 1975   301.18'5   74-12328
ISBN 0-398-03228-9
ISBN 0-398-03239-4 (pbk.)

Dedicated to Kevin and Lisa
Morris and Heather, Rachel and
Sheri Cinnamon, whose greatest
growth still lies ahead.

FOREWORD

IT IS UNUSUAL and may seem ungracious to ask in a Foreword whether or not the book should have been written.

Controversies about the harm or benefit of group procedures designed to enlighten, to train, to liberate emotions, and to alter consciousness have been endemic with and around what is often called the "human potential movement." Corporation officials disagree on the value of T-Groups for up-grading their managers. Religious leaders clash over weekend sensitivity groups for spiritual growth of their congregations. Educators engage in heated attacks and defenses of campus encounter groups. Some social scientists are critical and contemptuous; others are ardent advocates; most have some reservations.

The conflicts became much more acute after the founding of the Esalen Institute about 1960. William Schutz, especially, brought back to the N.T.L. summer workshops at Bethel, Maine, an enthusiasm for revolutionary new developments in group activities as practiced on the West Coast and a corresponding disparagement of the timid, conventional limitations of Eastern N.T.L. thinking and leadership. Non-verbal activities were at the heart of the controversy. Free expressions of affection and sexual interest were especially threatening to the more reserved and puritanical intellectuals; even more so when by men toward other males. Aggressive impulses, expressed by shouts, screams, pounding pillows, shoving, hand-wrestling and scuffles contrasted with accepted norms of calm rationality. The traditional group leaders viewed such new developments as "wild," "far out," and "dangerous." Indeed, the emotional casualties do seem to have increased with the more extreme styles of group direction. The best comparative study (Lieberman, Yalom, Miles, 1973) indicates that least harm came to participants in groups in which leaders were only moderate in degree of emotional stimulation, but generous in cognitive input—obviously largely verbal. On this basis, one may question whether a publication which may stimulate more risky behaviors by relatively inexperienced group trainers is desirable.

A second doubt arises from the rapid spread of all kinds of groups which allegedly facilitate personal growth. Some are led by competent psychologists and psychiatrists with considerable experience in diagnosing and treating personality problems. But many others are now being led by self-designated directors who have had very little sophisticated preparation. One hears of groups assembled by someone who has recently returned from one highly stimulating marathon or weekend and who can't wait to initiate his acquaintances. And, of course, there are the promoters who have found a way to easy money, exploiting the anxieties, life-frustrations, spiritual hungers and chronic dependencies so prolific in our society.

It seems likely that a manual of exercises will be especially sought by those group facilitators who have themselves had less training and experience. They want cookbooks; the established chefs can create their own recipes.

Despite these demurrers, I think Ken Morris and Ken Cinnamon are making a useful contribution. Withholding publication of the products of their good experience will not reduce the number of incompetents who enjoy seducing or bully-ragging members of their groups. There are, after all, far more would-be leaders who are genuinely concerned to provide interesting programs which help rather than hurt. Granted some self-discipline and a genuine concern for the welfare of others, the enlarged repertoire of activities will add to a trainer's effectiveness.

As more paraprofessionals become involved in community programs for mental health, the need for a manual like this becomes more evident. The paraprofessionals who are chosen to guide groups of young people, parents, or other adults, have usually been selected because of their own emotional stability, common sense and their good rapport with others. Most of them, however, have had only a limited range of group experiences and leadership training. This manual should prove exceptionally useful to them in suggesting activities.

The organization of the material under headings such as sensory awareness, relaxation and trust is likely to emphasize the fact that non-verbal exercises are not ends in themselves but means to the achievement of desirable insights and improved behavior. The mechanics of how an exercise is administered are less important than its pertinence to the purposes of the trainers or members.

The most important end which a manual of this kind can serve is to facilitate fresh inventions. Dr. Edward L. Thorndike, the distinguished educational psychologist, once wrote: "It is not necessity which is the mother of invention; the true mother of invention is knowledge of other people's inventions!" Here may be found the major contribution of this manual. After practitioners have tried several different exercises designed to sharpen sensory awareness and perception, for example, they may be ready to develop one of their own which will be more effective than any in this book. The best test of the value of this compilation is the extent to which it stimulates new and more useful inventions. If it results simply in more leaders using again and again the activities recommended here, the project would, in my eyes, be a failure. Its most useful role is that of a catalyst, enabling the emergence of other and even better suggestions for enriching the experience of group members. A good step in this direction might be to ask a group to read over all the exercises on some topic—perhaps "getting acquainted," to try out one or two; and then to devise an original exercise which will enable them to get better acquainted in more areas and with more depth than they would by the use of any or all the directions set forth here.

The latest volume of papers by Piaget bears the significant title: *To Understand is to Invent.* If this book is to be most productive, its use should not be limited to professional or amateur trainers. It should enable group members themselves to become more active in the processes of group growth and more creative in designing their own program. When the members take greater responsibility for what goes on in their group, the danger of dependence on, or exploitation by, an inadequate or perverted trainer is reduced. There will still be a need for a professional whose experience and wisdom can prevent group activities from being harmful to any participants. Our experience has been reassuring in this connection.

Group members have usually been quite protective—sometimes over-protective—of peers who are especially vulnerable. It appears most unlikely that the consensus of a group would approve an exercise for which some members are not yet ready. I think I would trust the group decision more than I would that of the average training practitioner on this point. But this is not an either-or situation. Both the members and the leader can participate in choosing and designing appropriate activities for a given stage of development in the group and its individual personalities. As members participate more intelligently in the selection and initiation of procedures which seem to meet their own recognized needs, the human potential movement will take a giant step forward.

GOODWIN WATSON

ACKNOWLEDGMENTS

THIS VOLUME, as is the case for most books, is the result of the aid and contributions of many persons.

We are unable to acknowledge everyone who assisted us, but we do wish to mention a few whose contributions were essential.

First, Goodwin Watson for his contributions, both literary and personal.

Second, Elayne Hunter, who took the Back Talk photographs.

Third, Roger Fultz, who is responsible for all the other photographs in this volume.

Fourth, Karen Koester, who carefully typed the manuscript and helped the authors by correcting their mistakes.

Fifth, Dan Millar, whose contribution of non-verbal exercises is deeply appreciated.

Sixth, Don Bertsch, Director of the Central Michigan University Counseling Center, for allowing us to use its facilities.

Seventh, the colleagues at the Central Michigan University Counseling Center for supporting us in our endeavors.

Eighth, Judy Morris, Dorothy, Molly and Sam Cinnamon, whose moral support was invaluable.

Last, and most important of the contributors, are all the members of our encounter, personal growth, marathon and t-groups. We learned from them and loved them. Without them and other group members, a volume such as this is unneeded.

K.T.M.
K.M.C.

INTRODUCTION

A FEW YEARS AGO, we noticed that the frequency of requests for and questions about group exercises directed at us was increasing. Almost weekly, someone would ask us which exercises they should use in devising a training workshop, running a t-group or for eliciting feedback, awareness, self-disclosure or some other group dynamic variable. Our first book was our way of answering their queries.[1]

However, that volume was only a partial answer, as it dealt only with verbal group exercises. This book completes our response to questions as to where group exercises can be found, how effective they can be and what goals they can meet.[2]

In this handbook the group facilitator will find 160 exercises and 85 exercise variations. No longer will he need to buy five or six volumes concerning group exercises. Instead, he can consult this volume when desiring a non-verbal group exercise and our previous volume (see footnote 1) when his needs dictate the use of a verbal group exercise.

The present volume offers the professional an opportunity to find specific exercises rapidly. For example, if he needs an exercise for getting acquainted, he simply opens the book to the chapter on Getting Acquainted and locates the exercise most in accord with his needs. If the wants to utilize an exercise in which Getting Acquainted is a subsidiary goal, he merely turns to the Index, discovers those exercises in which getting acquainted is a subsidiary goal,

---

[1]Morris, Kenneth T. and Kenneth M. Cinnamon. *A HANDBOOK OF VERBAL GROUP EXERCISES.* Charles C Thomas: Springfield, Illinois, 1974.

[2]Authors' Note: This handbook covers only non-verbal group exercises. A *non-verbal* exercise is defined as one in which 50 per cent or more of the member activity is non-verbal in nature.

examines them and chooses the one which most closely meets his needs.[3]

The advantages for the facilitator in using A HANDBOOK OF NON-VERBAL GROUP EXERCISES are many. We enumerate some of them as follows:

1. Each chapter has an introductory section which provides basic information on the use and appropriateness of each exercise under the (chapter) heading under consideration.
2. The order of main headings (i.e., chapter titles) under which the various exercises are listed, is alphabetical as well as numerical.
3. The goal for each exercise is clearly and specifically delineated.
4. Subsidiary goals are also listed for each exercise, again assuring the choice of an exercise appropriate to the facilitator's goal and subgoals.
5. A consistent format is used for every exercise, thereby facilitating application of the exercise and, from it, the development of *new* exercises. This type of format uniformity is sorely lacking in most volumes dealing with group exercises.
6. Clear indications are given concerning the group applicability of each exercise. Therefore, the practitioner needing an exercise suitable for an encounter group need only read the Group Application section of the exercise to determine its suitability for his purpose and group.
7. The ratio of non-verbal to verbal behavior is indicated in each case. Thus, the facilitator who wishes to use an exercise which contains some verbal interaction can easily discover the presence of such exercises.
8. Suggestions for processing are given, thereby aiding the facilitator in his procedure, analysis, and discussion efforts.
9. Dynamic, more effective exercises are marked with an *asterisk*.

---

[3]Authors' Note: There are many exercises marked with an asterisk (*). The asterisk indicates that the exercise has the potential to dynamically and most effectively meet the specified goal.

10. An extensive index is included, thereby easing access to exercises meeting the goal or subsidiary goals needed by the facilitator and/or his group. The presence of an index again differentiates this volume from others dealing with group exercises, since few books of such a nature include an index.

11. The handbook acquaints the facilitator with a multitude of non-verbal group exercises, thereby increasing his expertise.[4]

EXERCISE FORMAT

Each exercise is described, using a standardized format devised by the authors. We believe the format includes information on all the variables necessary for the facilitator to insure successful use of an exercise.

The reader will notice that usually the exercise goal is not indicated, except in the chapter on Ungrouped Exercises. The reason for this is that each exercise listed in any given chapter has that chapter's title as its specific goal. For example, all the exercises described in the chapter on Getting Acquainted have, as their specific goal, the elicitation of getting acquainted data.

The information included in the format sections within each Chapter is consistent from one exercise to another. Therefore, the facilitator does not have to read an entire exercise before he decides, for instance, its applicability and suitability for his group and for the group's particular requirements. He need only read the appropriate format sections of the exercise under consideration.

The format sections and an indication of the material included in each one follows:

SUBSIDIARY GOAL(S)—Herein are listed those subsidiary goals reached by the group utilizing the exercise.

The importance of subsidiary goals in a book dealing with non-verbal group exercises cannot be stressed enough. The primary goals for such exercises are noticeably fewer than those for verbal

---

[4]Authors' Note: Of course, the Handbook does not purport to cover *all* non-verbal group exercises, as such a task would be economically unfeasible. It does, however include a respresentative number of exercises, which are usable, effective, and congruent with the human relations area of group activity and endeavor.

exercises. For example, there are a preponderance of non-verbal group exercises whose primary goal is the increase of Sensory Awareness. However, the subsidiary goals do differ from one sensory awareness exercise to another. It is, therefore, *imperative* that the facilitator consider the subsidiary goals as being extremely important to exercise utilization and success. The Index lists *all* goals covered in this volume and indicates where they are primary or subsidiary in nature. Thus, the presence of the Index and utilizing it become of *paramount* importance.

GROUP APPLICATION—Each of these sections is written in such a manner that the facilitator rapidly develops insight into those groups with which the exercise may be used. Included, in the order of their appearance, are:

1. *Group size*—An indication of the size group with which the exercise may be utilized. We use twelve members or less for all encounter, personal growth, marathon and t-groups. The facilitator, if he has more than twelve members would be wise to modify the exercise in using it with his group.

2. *Types of groups which may utilize the exercise*—We have included the following groups for consideration with regard to application:

   a. *Encounter*—A group whose purposes are to help foster self-awareness and to help members establish genuine, authentic interpersonal relationships.

   b. *Personal growth*—A group whose purpose is to help the member grow and mature in his intrapersonal and interpersonal relationships. Particular emphasis is placed on growth as a feeling person.

   c. *Marathon*—A group whose purposes are, over an extended, concentrated period of twenty or more hours, to strip away member defenses so that interaction becomes more real, genuine and authentic.

   d. *T-group*—A group whose purposes are to bring about awareness of self as a group member, to create an intellectual awareness of group dynamics, and to build interpersonal skills which members can utilize in their everyday relationships.

e. *Problem solving*—A group whose purpose is to solve a problem or satisfactorily complete a task given to it. A subsidiary goal is to create awareness of member group roles.

f. *Classroom*—Herein we refer to *any* high school or college level classroom group of students. Utilization of exercises deemed suitable for the classroom with elementary classes should be carefully considered by the facilitator or group leader.

3. *Member experience and age*—Wherever the level of group members' experience or age is important to exercise success, comment is made.

4. *Sex ratio*—Where the ratio of males to females is important to exercise success, the facilitator is so informed.

APPLICATION VARIABLES—This section of the format includes the following data:

1. *TIME REQUIRED*—A statement of the time needed to conduct the exercise is indicated in each instance. Note that the time required refers only to *conducting* the exercise. It does not include an estimate of time needed for the facilitator to lead a discussion or to process the exercise, as the time spent on these activities is dependent on the needs of the group and on the facilitator's objectives.

2. *VERBAL AND NON-VERBAL RATIO*—The ratio between verbal and non-verbal activity for the exercise is indicated accordingly. We do this so that the facilitator desiring an exercise which does *not* include verbal activity, will be able to decide easily whether to utilize the exercise in question. In cases where the verbal behavior is a written activity, such is indicated.

3. *MATERIALS NEEDED*—Where materials are needed for an exercise, specific mention is made.

4. *ROOM SETTING*—Where a certain type of room setting is needed for exercise success, that is also noted.

ADMINISTRATIVE PROCEDURE—This section of the format contains step-by-step instructions to the facilitator regarding the proper administration of the exercise.

SUGGESTIONS FOR FACILITATOR PROCESS—Herein are contained a list of the questions the facilitator should use during the "processing" stage i.e. to effect the changes that will lead to the desired goal or result and to help make the exercise a learning experience. We realize we cannot include all the queries the facilitator will use during processing, but we have supplied a sufficient number of these not only to help make his processing productive, but also to suggest further questions the facilitator may develop.

VARIATIONS—For a sizable majority of the exercises, variations on the original exercise are available. We have included such variations for the facilitator, and we urge him to use these whenever he feels they will be more suitable to his group's requirements than will be the original exercise. We also urge the facilitator to develop *his own* variations or to alter any of the exercises in this book so that they may more appropriately meet his needs and those of his group.

Again we wish to emphasize *the asterisked exercises*. The authors and other professionals have discovered that the exercises which have thus been singled out possess above average potential in achieving the stated goal and subsidiary goals. However, because such exercises are more advanced and subtler, we do wish to caution that only the experienced facilitator should make use of them. Anxiety, frustration, feelings of rejection, and so forth, may in many cases be related to such dynamic exercises. Therefore, the facilitator utilizing them must be adept at processing and at helping members to cope with the feelings elicited by the particular activity. As the facilitator grows in expertise, he will wish to make greater use of exercises so designated.

HOW TO USE THE HANDBOOK

As we have pointed out, the facilitator will find that the Handbook is developed in such a way that he will have easy access to the exercise he desires. We have attempted to develop a more orderly approach to the exercise domain of human relations training than is presently available. The facilitator using this volume, will also appreciate the fact that he no longer need rely on the "hunt and find" effort required in other books dealing with group exercises.

For the most effective use of A HANDBOOK OF NON-VERBAL GROUP EXERCISES, we suggest that the facilitator approach it in the following fashion:

1. Decide what goal he wishes the needed exercise to meet.
2. Look for the appropriate chapter and/or use the Index at the back of the book to determine *which* exercises meet the goal in question.
3. Then, if certain variables are important to him, such as time required, materials needed, group size, etc., let him pay particular attention to the appropriate format sections of the exercise under consideration.
4. After following the above steps, the facilitator will have one or more exercises at his disposal. He may then choose whichever of these he deems most appropriate for his particular group, *or* he may use an asterisked exercise, knowing *beforehand* that the exercise chosen has definite potential for meeting the goal in question.

Exercise Sources

We have given credit to exercise designers wherever such credit was necessary or appropriate. We could not give credit for each exercise, for the majority have reached us by word of mouth or are fifth- and sixth-hand versions of exercises developed by unknown contributors to the field of group interaction. We have discovered that the majority of our exercises existed in people's heads, on scraps of notebook paper, on unsigned handouts, etc. We have not copied any known copyrighted material without the copyright owner's permission.

Concluding Comments

In this volume we have set out to develop a handbook of nonverbal group exercises that is easy for the facilitator to use, presents him with a wealth of readily accessible new material, provides all the necessary information as to various aspects of these exercises, offers the facilitator ease of duplication and application, and—hopefully—furthers the professional and public stature of the human relationships training field. We believe we have been successful in these efforts.

Lay Use Versus Professional Use

Non-verbal group exercises can be extremely potent as learning tools. They can also be frightening, awesome and overwhelming for many participants. They can be these things because they "take away" man's most used tool, his *words*. Simply not being able to speak can lead to an experience which is highly positive and beneficial or negative and non-educative. Whether a non-verbal experience *is* rewarding depends heavily on the facilitator and his expertise. He must be accurate in his assessment of the members' readiness for a non-verbal exercise and accurate in his assessment of the group's needs.

We make these comments not so much for the professional as for the "layman." Many of these exercises can be used by the non-professional. And, since sensory awareness is an "in" thing nowadays, we assume that many laymen will attempt these exercises. However, we would like to caution them concerning their attempts to use such exercises in their everyday group situations.

We do not propose that this book be a guide to Everyman's group efforts. It is designed for use by professional group facilitators and group leaders. Laymen, if they wish to conduct an exercise, should restrict themselves to those exercises listed as "applicable to any group," still using caution. This is not a party book, nor a "game" and "gimmick" book for instant self-growth. It is a professional effort to be used by experienced professionals. Regardless of who uses the book, *any* exercise is to be regarded as a tool rather than as an end in itself.

CONTENTS

A HANDBOOK OF NON-VERBAL
GROUP EXERCISES

I

COPING

THE PRIMARY GOAL for each exercise in this chapter is to expose each member to his coping behavior and to help him investigate his own ability to cope with varied feelings, thoughts and reactions. The question we ask here is this: How does the individual member non-verbally cope with a variety of experimental situations?

Within the coping chapter, the reader will find a number of primary goals i.e. coping with anger, coping with frustration, coping with the here-and-now. The facilitator should select the coping exercise which is most appropriate for the group in its particular stage of development. For example, if the group appears to be having difficulty coping with anger, the facilitator would use an exercise designed to elicit anger and expose the members to their "coping with anger" behaviors.

Coping exercises are appropriate, in most instances, *only* for encounter, personal growth, marathon and t-groups. This chapter is differentiated from other chapters by the fact that recognition of the coping mechanisms is the important factor. In other words, the facilitator is not so interested in exposing the group to the feelings of "anger" as he is interested in getting them to recognize and investigate how they *cope* (or fail to cope) with anger.

The dynamics which are elicited by coping exercises can be of great benefit as learning tools to both the group and its individual members. However, since they are non-verbal, the members *must* be allowed the opportunity to discuss them. Such discussion helps alleviate any anxieties, frustrations, angers etc. which might result from the exercise. It is obvious, therefore, that the processing stage is a must. The facilitator should use it in *all* instances. It will help eliminate any feelings which are "gunny sacked" and also help make the exercise a learning experience.

3

Coping with Acceptance

*TRY TO ESCAPE[1]

Subsidiary Goal(s)
a. To develop group unity.
b. To develop feelings of warmth and acceptance among the members.

Group Application
Twelve members or less. To be used only with encounter, personal growth, marathon and t-groups whose members have developed rapport between and insight into each other.

Application Variables
Two to five minutes. The exercise is 100% non-verbal.

Administrative Procedure
a. Whenever the facilitator notices that a member appears to feel rejected by the group, to perceive himself as not being a part of them, or to feel that others view him negatively, the facilitator has him enter the center of the circle.
b. He tells the member: "You appear to feel not a part of us. Yet, you are. In order to show you this, we are going to encircle you. Your job is to break out."
c. He tells the others: "Those of you who feel that (name the member) *is* a part of our group and who want him to *be* a part of it form a circle around him. Hold each others' waists tightly. Make the circle a strong chain which he cannot break. Do your best to keep him in the circle."
d. The facilitator joins the circle. He then tells the member: "Try to escape. Break out of the enclosure. We, who want you there, who want you to be part of us, will do our best to keep you inside."

---

[1]Although this exercise is frequently used to illustrate the dynamics of rejection, the authors have discovered that it is far more dynamic when used to illustrate how unrelenting acceptance can be.

e. After the member succeeds or ceases his efforts the facilitator and the others give the member a group hug.* The experience is then discussed.

Suggestions for Facilitator Process

Concentrate on the following during processing:

a. *To the member:* How did you feel as you tried to break out? Why do you think we resisted your escape so vigorously?

Figure 5-1. Group Hug.

---

[1]A group hug consists of the members circling the member, moving in on him with arms spread, and hugging him *simultaneously*.

Figure 5-2. Group Hug.

Point out: if we didn't want you with us, we would have allowed you an easy escape. How do you feel now about you as a part of us?

b. *To the others:* How did you feel during the escape attempt? Did you *let* him escape? If yes, why? If not, why not? (Usually, the members resisted because they wanted the member to get the message "we want you here and we'll do our best to keep you here.") How do you feel now about the member?

c. Ask any members who did not participate why they chose to watch instead of involve themselves.

Figure 5-3. Group Hug.

Variations
    None

                                                    Coping with Anger
                        CONNECTING DOTS
Subsidiary Goal(s)
    a. To recognize how one copes with frustration.
    b. To recognize how one copes with anxiety.
    c. To determine how well members listen.
    d. To determine how one copes with authority.

Group Application

Twenty members or less, although most ideally suited for groups of eight to twelve. Applicable to any group. When twenty or more are present, use the Teamwork exercise found in this chapter.

Application Variables

Ten to twenty minutes. The exercise is 100 per cent non-verbal. Paper and pencils for each member are needed.

Administrative Procedure

a. The facilitator tells the members: "Take your paper and pencil out. Now, place dots on the paper. You can put as many or as few dots on the paper as you wish. This is to be done non-verbally. You are not to talk to each other."

b. When all members have completed the assignment, the facilitator continues: "Now, connect the dots. Be sure your connecting line does not cross itself."

c. As the members are engaged in the connecting dots phase, the facilitator moves around the room. He peers at the drawings, mutters angrily about people not following directions, laughs at some of the efforts, etc. He is to give the impression that he is angry and displeased.

d. After all have finished, the facilitator says: "Let's do it again. This time, do it right." He then repeats step *a* and *b*.

e. During the second task, the facilitator sits quietly until all members have finished. He then leads a discussion of the experience, first explaining that his anger was feigned.

Suggestions for Facilitator Process

Concentrate on the following during processing:

a. How did you feel when you discovered I was angry with your first performance? What feelings about me did you have?

b. Did your first and second drawings differ with regard to the number of dots you put down? Why?

c. What have you learned about your means of coping with authority, anger, frustration and anxiety?

Variations

Variation I

a. Decide ahead of time which *one* member's performance you will pretend to be pleased by.

b. Conduct the exercise as in its original form. *However,* during phase *c,* make sure the group is aware of the fact that one member is "doing it right."

c. Now say: "Let's do it again. This time do it right." Tell the member you were pleased with to "show the others how it's done."

d. After the second task, discuss the experience stressing the feelings aroused toward you and the member you were pleased with and whether members tried to imitate his drawing. Investigate the reasons for members' changing (or not changing) the second drawing.

Variation II

a. Decide ahead of time which one member you will be displeased with.

b. Conduct the exercise as before, but exhibit pleasure for every drawing *except* that of the member chosen.

c. Do not repeat the drawing. Instead, process, stressing the chosen member's feelings and the feelings that other members had toward him, you, and themselves.

*FIGHT EACH OTHER!

Subsidiary Goal(s)

a. To give and receive feedback.
b. To explore the dynamics of bodily awareness.
c. To learn how to constructively confront.
d. To explore the dynamics involved in creative combat.

Group Application

Twelve members or less. Since dyads are used, group size should be even. To be used with encounter, personal growth, marathon and t-groups. Best results are obtained if the group members have had some previous exposure to constructive confrontation.

Application Variables

Twenty to thirty minutes. The exercise is 50 per cent non-verbal and 50 per cent verbal. The room must be large enough to allow the members unrestrained movement.

Administrative Procedure

a. The facilitator gives the following introduction: "In our everyday lives it is often difficult to confront people constructively. I would like you to non-verbally pair off with another member whom you have wanted to confront but haven't or have some ambiguous feelings toward."

b. After all members have paired off, the facilitator states: "Spread out within the room. When I say begin I want you to begin to wrestle with one another. The only rule is that all physical movements must be done in *slow motion*. Feel free to exaggerate blows, slaps, kicks, etc. Make sure you do not touch your partner with any force. React to the blows in slow motion. Please begin."

c. After ten minutes, the facilitator asks the dyads to stop fighting and to sit down with one another and discuss the experience.

d. When the facilitator senses that all dyads have had an opportunity to fully discuss the experience, the dyads regroup for processing.

Suggestions for Facilitator Process

Concentrate on the following during processing:

a. What have you learned about your partner? How vicious did your fighting become? What insights about yourself have you gained from the experience?

b. Where did you repeatedly hit your partner? Was it difficult to keep all of your movements in slow motion? Why? Have your feelings changed toward your partner? If so, in what way? Why not?

Variations

*Variation I

a. If two members are having difficulty confronting one an-

other, have them enter the middle of the circle and fight using *only* slow motion movements.
b. When done, have the two members discuss their experience in the middle of the large circle.

*TAKE THAT!

Subsidiary Goal(s)
   a. To give and receive feedback.
   b. To become more aware of non-verbal cues.
   c. To learn to constructively handle anger.
   d. To open hidden agendas.
   e. To explore the dynamics involved in dominance and submission.

Group Application

Twelve members or less. To be used with encounter, personal growth, marathon and t-groups. The exercise is intended to be used with groups whose developmental growth has been hampered by hidden agendas of anger or frustration.

Application Variables

Fifteen to twenty minutes. The exercise is 100 percent non-verbal. The room must be large enough to allow the members to spread out without feeling unduly restricted.

Administrative Procedure

   a. The facilitator asks members to non-verbally form dyads with members toward whom they have neutral or negative feelings.
   b. The facilitator then says: "Remain standing with the taller member's hands on the shoulders of the smaller members. When I say begin, the taller member is to try to force the smaller member down by pushing on his shoulders. Try to push your partner to his knees."
   c. After several minutes, the facilitator says: "Stop. Help your partner up. Reverse roles and repeat the process."

d. After step *c* has been completed, the members discuss the experience.

Suggestions for Facilitator Process

Concentrate on the following during processing:

a. What feelings did you have toward your partner? Did you become angry? How did you cope with it? How much physical energy did you actually exert?

b. What were you aware of during the exercise? What messages was your body sending to you? Have your feelings changed toward your partner? If so, in what way? Why have they changed?

Variations

*Variation I

a. If the group is having extreme difficulty with one member in terms of his or their anger or frustration, the facilitator asks that member to step into the middle of the large circle.

b. All other members place their hands on his shoulders and force him down. Then the group is to help lift him up.

c. Processing should concentrate on the extent to which the physical struggle alleviated the anger and frustration, changes in feelings between the member and the group and reason for such changes.

*TEAMWORK

Subsidiary Goal(s)

a. To learn how groups operate when non-verbally completing a task.

b. To investigate member roles.

c. To determine how one copes with authority.

Group Application

Twenty to fifty members. The exercise is most effective when used with groups of twenty to thirty. Subgroups are used, so the group size should be such that subgroups of four and/or five can be formed. Applicable to any group.

Application Variables

Fifteen to thirty minutes. The exercise is 100 per cent non-verbal. Two pieces of paper per subgroup and pencils for all members are needed. The room must be large enough to allow the subgroups ample room in which to work.

Administrative Procedure

a. The facilitator says: "Non-verbally, arrange yourself in subgroups of (state desired number) ."
b. He tells the subgroups to find a spot in the room and sit in a circle.
c. He places two pieces of paper and a sufficient number of pencils in the center of each subgroup's circle.
d. The facilitator says: "The task for your subgroups is to place dots on *one* piece of paper. There can be as many or as few dots on the paper as you wish. This is to be done non-verbally. You are not to talk to each other."
e. When all subgroups have finished, the facilitator continues: "Now, connect the dots. Be sure your connecting line does not cross itself."
f. As the subgroups are engaged in the task, the facilitator moves around the room. He looks at each subgroup's drawings, mutters angrily about people not following orders, laughs at some of the efforts, etc. He is to give the impression that he is angry and displeased.
g. After all have finished, he says: "Let's do it again. This time, do it right." He then repeats step *d* and *e*.
h. During the second task, the facilitator sits quietly until all subgroups have finished. He then explains that his anger was feigned and leads a discussion of the experience.

Suggestions for Facilitator Process

Concentrate on the following during processing:
a. What feelings toward me did you have when you discovered I was angry with your first performance? What feelings did you have toward each other?
b. How did the subgroup accomplish the first task? How did

the accomplishment of the second task differ from the first? Why?

c. What roles did you see yourself and others engage in? Did roles differ between task one and two? Why?

Variations

Variation I

a. Decide ahead of time which *one* subgroup's performance you will pretend to be pleased by.

b. Conduct the exercise as in its original form. *However,* during phase *f,* make sure the subgroups are aware of the fact that one subgroup is "doing it right."

c. Now say: "Let's do it again. This time do it right. You may look at (name the subgroup who did it right) drawing."

d. After the second task, discuss the experience stressing the feelings aroused toward you and the subgroup you were pleased by and whether the other subgroups tried to imitate their drawing. Investigate the reasons for the subgroups' changing (or not changing) the second drawing.

Variation II

a. Decide ahead of time which one subgroup you will show displeasure to.

b. Conduct the exercise as before, but exhibit pleasure for every drawing *except* that of the subgroup chosen.

c. Do not repeat the drawing. Instead, process, stressing the chosen subgroup members' feelings and the feelings the other subgroup members had toward them, you, and themselves.

Coping with Anxiety

*SHELTER

Subsidiary Goal(s)

a. To explore the dynamics involved in security.

b. To help members gain greater insight into coping with anxiety.

c. To facilitate the process of fantasy.

Group Application

Twelve members or less. To be used with encounter, personal growth, marathon and t-groups. Caution should be exercised if this exercise is used before the group members have had ample time to have developed a trustful, supportive atmosphere.

Application Variables

Thirty minutes. The exercise is 100 per cent non-verbal. The room must be large enough to allow members unrestricted movement.

Administrative Procedure

a. The facilitator makes the following introduction: "Awareness of our anxieties and how we resolve them is a very important dynamic in our daily lives. This exercise is designed to give us greater awareness into how we deal with tension and anxiety. I would like you to spread out within the room and to lie on your back with your eyes closed."

b. After all members have spread out, the facilitator continues: "Think of an incident which made you feel extremely anxious. As you do this, tense your body as tightly as possible and then relax. Do this several times. Tense up, relax, tense up, relax. As you are doing this, try and become aware of the changes in feelings occurring in your body."

c. After five to ten minutes, the facilitator says: "Lie back and relax. Fantasize that you are enclosed in a protective blanket. Assume any position which you feel comfortable with and secure in. Let yourself feel the warmth and security of your "security" blanket."

d. After five to ten minutes, the facilitator says: "Slowly unwrap yourself from your protective blanket. Do this physically. Move as if you were coming out from under a large, secure, encompassing blanket. Take your time. When you are ready, please form a circle and we will join for processing."

Suggestions for Facilitator Process

Concentrate on the following during processing:

a. What did you do when you felt the initial anxiety? What was your body saying to you? What else were you aware of?
b. What differences did you notice between relaxing and tensing? Does this have any bearing on the way you handle everyday problems? If so, in what way?
c. How did you feel about your security blanket? What thoughts and images passed through your mind? What insights have you gained?

Variations

None

Coping with Closeness

*CRAWL TO CLOSENESS

Subsidiary Goal(s)

a. To develop insight into one's feelings about touching and being touched.
b. To learn to observe another's body language.

Group Application

Twenty members or less. Since dyads are used, the group size should be even. To be used with encounter, personal growth, marathon and t-groups during the early stages of development.

Application Variables

Five to ten minutes. The exercise is 100 per cent non-verbal. The room must be large enough to allow the dyads to be sufficiently removed from each other to insure a sense of privacy. The room should also be carpeted. Each dyad will require ten feet of space. Therefore, the exercise should not be used if such space is not available.

Administrative Procedure

a. The facilitator asks that the members non-verbally form dyads. He asks that "you try to pick a partner who you do not know too well."

b. He then tells the dyads: "Find a spot in the room where you feel comfortable. Then sit on the floor. Allow ten feet of space between you and your partner."

c. When the dyads are seated, the facilitator says: "Look across at your partner. Try to determine in yourself how close you feel to him. Look at his non-verbal behavior. Use it to determine how close you are to him."

d. After a minute he says: "Crawl toward your partner. Crawl as close to him as you wish. If you wish, remain distant from him. Let the distance represent your closeness to him.

Try to determine what the other person is saying to you. Is he saying touch me or leave me alone? Does he want you close or far? Feel what his body is saying and react to it.

When you feel your crawl and its accompanying conversation is finished, rejoin the original circle and we will discuss this experience."

Suggestions for Facilitator Process

Concentrate on the following during processing:

a. How did you feel at the start of the exercise? What did your partner do during the stage before I told you to crawl to each other that told you how close he felt to you?

b. How did you feel during the crawling stage? How did you show your feelings of closeness? Who touched each other? Why? Who did not? Why not?

c. What have you learned about yourself concerning touch and closeness? What have you learned about your partner? Do you feel closer to your partner now? If yes, why? If no, why not?

Variations

*Variation I

a. Whenever the facilitator notices that the group is having difficulty communicating with a member, especially in terms of warmth and closeness, he has the member sit in the middle of the group circle.

b. He then tells the others: "Expand the circle so that we are ten feet from this member."

c. He continues: "Now, each of us is to crawl to this member. Let the distance between you and him represent how close you feel to him."

d. When the group crawl is finished, the facilitator processes the exercise, concentrating on differences in distance, the reasons for the differences in feelings of closeness for the member, and the member and groups' reaction to the experience.

*ENCLOSURE[1]

Subsidiary Goal(s)

a. To experience feelings of personal threat and anxiety.

Group Application

Twelve to twenty members. Applicable to any group.

Application Variables

Three minutes per participant. The exercise is 100 per cent nonverbal. The corners of the room must be accessible.

Administrative Procedure

a. The facilitator asks for a volunteer who is willing to investigate his need for personal space. The volunteer is told to place himself in one of the corners of the room.

b. The rest of the members are placed in the corner *opposite* the volunteer and told: "En masse, slowly advance toward the volunteer until you "crush" him into the corner."

c. After step *b*, process. The exercise can be represented until all who wish it have had the opportunity.

Suggestions for Facilitator Process

Concentrate on the following during processing:

a. *To the volunteer:* What feelings were you aware of? How

---

[1]Adapted from an exercise developed by Dan Millar, Coordinator of Interpersonal and Public Communication, Central Michigan University.

did you cope with them? Did the intensity of your feelings change as the group approached? Why?

b. *To the group advancing:* What were your feelings and emotions as you neared the volunteer? What were your thoughts and feelings about the volunteer?

Variations

*Variation I

a. During step *b* of the original exercise, tell the volunteer: "Stop the group's advance when they have come too close for your comfort."

b. After the volunteer has stopped the group's advance, the facilitator says to him: "Take some time to become aware of your feelings."

c. After a minute, the facilitator tells the advancing group: "Start advancing. Keep advancing until you "crush" the volunteer into the corner."

d. During processing, concentrate on the volunteer's and advancing group's feelings during the three stages of initial advance, stoppage and crushing advance.

Variation II

a. Increase the size of the volunteers. Then repeat the initial exercise.

b. During processing, concentrate on whether having company in the corner changed the intensity of the emotion and feelings aroused.

*Variation III

a. Use *only* members who identify themselves as needing large personal space areas.

b. Place them, one at a time, in a corner and repeat the original exercise.

LINES

Subsidiary Goal(s)

a. To give and receive feedback.
b. To gain insight into members' perceptions.
c. To gain greater awareness of non-verbal cues.

Group Application

Twelve members or less. Since dyads are used, group size should be even. To be used with encounter, personal growth, marathon and t-groups. Best results are obtained if the exercise is used in the initial stages of the group's life.

Application Variables

Ten to fifteen minutes. The exercise is 100 per cent non-verbal. The room must be large enough to allow the group members unrestrained movement.

Administrative Procedure

a. The facilitator presents the following introduction: "Frequently we pass over other people's lines of intimacy without being aware of it. Confrontation of one's range of comfort can be a valuable, insight filled experience."

b. The facilitator then asks the group to form two lines against two opposite walls, with each member facing a partner across the room.

c. The facilitator makes the following statement: "When I say begin I would like you to start moving very slowly toward your partner. Become aware of how you are adapting to your partner's pace. Get as close as you can without crossing over your partner's line of intimacy. Remember not to violate your own or your partner's comfort range. When you reach a point of mutual agreement, stop."

d. After all members have stopped the group members, process the experience.

Suggestions for Facilitator Process

Concentrate on the following during processing:

a. How did you decide on which partner to choose? What type of non-verbal cues were you aware of? What feedback were you receiving and sending?

b. At what point did you decide to stop? Do you feel anyone crossed over your line of intimacy? If yes, how did you cope with this? Do you feel you passed over anyone's line of intimacy? How did he cope with it?

Variations

None

Coping with Frustration

*DEAF

Subsidiary Goal(s)

a. To develop sensory awareness.
b. To learn the role sterotyping plays in analysis of a visualized phenomenon.

Group Application

Twelve members or less. To be used with encounter, personal growth, marathon and t-groups. The exercise is most effective when used in the middle stages of the group's life.

Application Variables

Time is unlimited, depending upon the length of the film viewed. The exercise is (usually) 60 per cent non-verbal and 40 per cent verbal, again depending on the film viewed. A film, videotape or television is needed. (See Administrative Procedure, step *a*). If a film or tape are chosen, the equipment necessary to monitor them is also needed. The room must be able to be darkened for *clear* viewing of the screen, monitor or television.

Administrative Procedure

a. Prior to the start of the session, the facilitator selects a film or videotape of his choosing. If these are not available, a television should be used.

Although longer running programs are usable, the facilitator should attempt to choose a film or videotape which runs thirty to sixty minutes. The program chosen should, hopefully, be one in which action and dialogue are evenly dispersued. For example, situation comedies and westerns tend to have too much action, while panel shows have too much talk.

The facilitator wants to show the members a film, tape or television program which would tend to elicit an emotional reaction, *but* which no member has seen.

Films	*Videotapes*	*Television*
Sunshine	Check the audio-	Check your
Brian's Song	visual department	local
David and Lisa	at the local	television
Love Story	library.	programming
A Journey Into Self		guide.
(Carl Rogers)		

b. When the group arrives, the facilitator says: "We are going to take the opportunity today to learn how much we rely on our hearing and how little we rely on our other senses. Hopefully, we will learn a little bit more about our unused senses.

I am going to show you a (film, videotape, television program). However, I will turn the sound *off*. You should try to use your other senses, your brain and your "guts" to determine what is going on in the program.

Try to determine what is happening. Try to determine why it is occurring. Try to empathize with the characters. There is to be *no* verbal communication from this point on."

c. The facilitator then shows the selection. After it is over, he asks that the members share their insights, views and analyses of the program.

d. After step *c* is completed, the facilitator tells the members about the selection. The members then discuss the experience.

Suggestions for Facilitator Process

Concentrate on the following during processing:

a. Who most accurately guessed what the selection meant? *To those members:* How did you do this? What senses did you use? What physical cues did you hone in on?

b. Who was least accurate? *To those members:* Why were you

unable to function without your ears? How do you feel about your inaccuracy?

c. *To all:* What have you learned about yourself? About your senses? Which senses are you now more aware of? Why? How did you cope with your frustrations?

Variations

None

*FLOODING

Subsidiary Goal(s)

a. To gain insight into one's reaction to sensory abuse.

Group Application

Twelve members or less. To be used with encounter, personal growth, marathon and t-groups after the members have developed some feeling of group unity.

Application Variables

Five to ten minutes per participant. The exercise will lose effectiveness if repeated more than three times. The exercise is 100 per cent non-verbal for each volunteer, although some talking will occur between other members. A radio, television, record player, horns, paper bags and other noise making devices are needed. A one or two page handout describing feedback, self-disclosure or some other group dynamic is also needed.

Administrative Procedure

a. The facilitator says: "I would like a volunteer who is willing to test his level of frustration."

b. The volunteer is asked to leave the room. The facilitator then tells the others: "When the volunteer returns, I will give him a handout which describes an aspect of group dynamics. I will tell him he is to read and digest it so that he can report as fully as possible its content to us.

You are to give him a minute to get settled. After that time, play the radio, turn on the record player, blow up and break the paper bags, blow the horns, make noise. In other words, flood the volunteer with outside sound. Talk to each other and to him. Keep the noise loud and continuous until I or the volunteer stops you."

c. The volunteer is returned to the room and given his assignment.

d. After five minutes or when it becomes apparent to the facilitator that the volunteer is too frustrated, the exercise is stopped. Processing should occur immediately.

e. After processing, the exercise can be repeated with a new volunteer.

Suggestions for Facilitator Process

Concentrate on the following during processing:

a. *To the volunteer:* Tell us about the handout. Seldom will he be able to relate much of what he read. Ask him why? How did you feel? How did you cope with your anger and frustration? Were you successful? If not, why not? What sensory abuse were you most aware of?

b. *To the others:* Did the noise bother you? Why? Why not? How did you feel about your roles? How did you cope with your feelings?

Variations

None

*GLOVE REMOVAL

Subsidiary Goal(s)

a. To learn how one reacts to success or failure.

Group Application

Group size is unlimited, although processing is difficult with groups of twenty or more. Applicable to any group.

Application Variables

Five minutes. The exercise is 100 per cent non-verbal. One glove for each member is required. The glove should not be skin tight. Nor should it be so loose fitting that it can be easily removed. A glove $\frac{1}{2}$ to one size larger than the individual usually wears will prove ideal.

Administrative Procedure

a. The facilitator gives a glove to each member. He then says: "Using only the hand on which the glove fits, put the glove on. Wiggle into it." (This fitting procedure *will* work. The facilitator may wish to demonstrate.).

b. After all have succeeded (or given up), the facilitator says: "Fit the glove on your hand.
You will have five minutes to wiggle out of the glove. Get it off. However, do not use your other hand, teeth or any other body part. Go."

c. After five minutes, the facilitator says: "Remove the glove and we will discuss this experience." (Seldom will anyone have been able to remove the glove.).

Suggestions for Facilitator Process

Concentrate on the following during processing:

a. How did it feel to succeed in wiggling into the glove? How did it feel to fail?

b. How did you feel as you tried to remove the glove? How did you cope with your feelings of anger, futility and frustration? Were you successful in your coping? If not, why not?

c. If any succeeded, ask them how they did it and how it felt to succeed where most of the others failed.

Variations

None

Coping with Here-and-Now

*HERE-THERE-EVERYWHERE

Subsidiary Goal(s)

a. To explore the dynamics involved in fantasy.

b. To gain greater insight into bodily awareness.

c. To explore members' time and space orientation.

Group Application

Twelve members or less. To be used with any group interested in exploring the relationship between the here and now as compared to the there and then.

Application Variables

Ten minutes. The exercise is 100 per cent non-verbal.

Administrative Procedure

a. The facilitator may wish to give a brief lecturette about the importance of being able to differentiate between the here and now and the there and then.

b. He then asks each member to look around and to become *aware* of the physical surroundings in the room.

c. After a few minutes, the facilitator says: "Close your eyes and withdraw by fantasizing any experience or place of your choosing."

d. Again, after a few minutes, the facilitator says: "Open your eyes and focus your awareness on the differences between where you just were and where you are now."

e. Steps *a* through *d* are repeated once more.

f. The members then discuss the experience.

Suggestions for Facilitator Process

Concentrate on the following during processing:

a. What types of fantasies did you have when you withdrew from the here and now? Where did you go? Why? What have you discovered about your own pattern of behavior as it relates to withdrawing from the here and now?

b. Were you aware of the changes your body was going through as you opened and closed your eyes? What were you most aware of in the here and now? Why?

c. How do you feel this simple experiment can be used to gain greater awareness of yourself? Do you feel this process of withdrawal plays an important part in your own avoidance behavior?

Variations

None

II

FANTASY

THE PRIMARY GOAL for each exercise in this chapter is the exploration of the fantasy process. This is accomplished by eliciting fantasy material.

This chapter differs from other chapters found in this book in that Subsidiary Goal(s), Group Application and Application Varibles have been generalized to encompass all of the exercises described. Special instructions, when needed for a fantasy exercise, are included. Variations are also indicated. The extent of nonverbal to verbal interaction and the length of time required for the members to reach full potency with a fantasy exercise are *not* indicated. These are omitted because time and interaction ratios will differ from group to group. Obviously, the facilitator *must* know his group members before deciding on utilizing any fantasy exercise.

As has been indicated above, fantasy exercises are contingent upon the facilitator's discretion. It is *his* perceptions which determine the appropriateness of any particular fantasy experience. It is *he* who determines when the members will move from one stage to another during the exercise. It is because of these factors that we recommend that only experienced facilitators use the following exercises.

Fantasy exercises can greatly enhance and deepen one's introspective abilities and interpersonal relationships. Relaxation, an anxiety free atmosphere and a significant level of trust are desirable for effective use of fantasy exercises. It is because of this that we suggest that before the facilitator employs a fantasy exercise, he assures himself that the group has had sufficient sessions for a climate of cohesiveness and trust to have developed.

All of the following fantasy exercises will be more effective if the facilitator takes the time to help each member attain a steady level of relaxation before he initiates the fantasy. A warm up is therefore recommended. During the warm up, the members should sit or recline in a comfortable position, close their eyes, and breathe evenly and deeply. The facilitator should urge them to "relax."

There are virtually an endless amount of fantasy exercises. Similarly, there are numerous variations to most fantasy exercises. Instead of attempting to delineate these lists of exercises, we have decided to limit the entries to nineteen fantasy exercises. We encourage the facilitator to create his own fantasy exercises and variations, using our entries as guidelines to the various forms of the fantasy process. As an example, the Western Town fantasy may be easily adapted to a number of other settings (e.g. a zoo, a pioneer town, a cave man camp, etc.). The process will remain essentially the same, while the change in setting may make significant differences in the insights gained and awarenesses discovered.

FANTASY EXERCISE FORMAT

Subsidiary Goal(s)

    a. To gain greater insight into members' cognitive processes.

    b. To further explore the process of creativity and spontaneity.

    c. To enhance and increase members' perceptive abilities.

    d. To achieve greater self-insight.

    e. To promote the feeling of closeness and cohesiveness.

Group Application

Twelve members or less. Applicable to any group, but more often used in encounter, personal growth, marathon and t-groups. Best results are obtained if the following exercises are used in advanced stages of the group's life, although they may be adapted for integration during the earlier stages of the group's life.

Application Variables

Time will vary according to the length of time needed to achieve the process of fantasy. Most of the following exercises will run from thirty minutes to one hour. The exercises contain a minimum of 50 per cent non-verbal content. The room should be large enough to allow members to move about unrestrained.

ANIMAL JOURNEY

Administrative Procedure

a. The facilitator asks the members to spread out within the room. He then gives the following instructions: "I want you to close your eyes and imagine an animal which you feel comfortable with."

b. After several minutes the facilitator continues: "I want you to imagine the animal's surroundings. Try to get in touch with the animal's needs and desires."

c. After several more minutes the facilitator states: "I now want you to become that animal. Try to associate yourself with its movements, posture, and temperament. If you feel comfortable doing so, I would like you to physically assume your animal's posture."

d. After a few minutes, the facilitator says: "Slowly come out of your fantasy. Leave your imagined animal and become yourself."

e. The members then discuss the experience.

Suggestions for Facilitator Process

Concentrate on the following during processing:

a. What animal did you become? Why? Did your choice of animals change through the experience? What type of surroundings did you chose?

b. Did you feel you actually became your animal? If not, why not? If so, what type of feelings did this arouse? What type of temperament did you assume?

CORNERS

Administrative Procedure

a. The facilitator asks each member to look around the room and to find a corner of the room to concentrate on. (Each of the following steps should occur in five minute intervals).

b. Members are then told: "Mentally place a person of your choice in the corner."

c. The facilitator continues: "Fantasize the surroundings and environment around your person."

d. He says: "Bring more people into the corner. Fantasize the type of action and interaction taking place."

e. After five minutes, the members discuss the experience.

Suggestions for Facilitator Process

Concentrate on the following during processing:

a. Who did you place in your corner? What environment did you later evoke? Did your fantasy have any special meaning for you? What was its meaning?

b. What activity took place in your fantasy? Did you find it difficult to fantasize during any stage of the exercise? When and why?

Variations

*Variation I

a. During step *b*, the facilitator says: "Mentally place a member of this group in the corner."

b. Step *c* of the original exercise now occurs.

c. The facilitator then says: "Bring more group members into the corner. Fantasize the type of action and interaction which is taking place."

d. The exercise continues as in its original form.

CRAYONS

Administrative Procedure

a. The facilitator passes around several sheets of drawing paper and crayons to each member in the group.

b. He then says: "Draw a fantasy picture. Try to let it emerge without prior thought or conscious direction. Try to let the drawing shape itself. You will have thirty minutes."

c. After thirty minutes, each member is urged to explain and discuss with the rest of the group his fantasy picture. Members are asked to share impressions, feelings, and reactions to the drawings.

d. When all who wish to describe and talk about their picture have had the opportunity to do so, the members discuss the experience.

Suggestions for Facilitator Process

Concentrate on the following during processing:

a. Do you feel you were able to "let go" with your drawing and let it flow spontaneously? Were you surprised at the results? Why? What have you learned about yourself?

b. What feelings did you have toward other members' drawings? What insights have you gained about the other members in the group?

Variations

Variation I

a. Instruct the members to draw "death" and "life."

b. Repeat basic format.

*EMOTIONS—HAPPY AND SAD

Administrative Procedure

a. The facilitator asks the members to spread out within the room and, while standing up, to close their eyes.

b. The facilitator then gives the following instructions: "I would like you all to stand in a comfortable position and allow your body to relax. Let your arms hang limp, let your facial muscles drop, let your stomach muscles relax and breathe slowly and deeply."

c. After several minutes the facilitator says: "I want you to recall a situation that hurt you. I would like you to reexperience this situation. Feel free to express what you are feeling with your entire body."

d. When the facilitator feels that all or most of the members have attained a point of experiencing the memory fully, he adds: "I would now like you to deal with that feeling of hurt, as defensively or openly as possible. Feel free to strike out or to hold yourself, whatever you feel the most comfortable with."

e. After several minutes the facilitator gives the following instructions: "I now want you to fantasize about the most beautiful day you could conceive of. Try to picture the weather, your surroundings, etc. When you are able to feel this day completely, I want you to express the joy and elation that you feel."

f. After several minutes, the facilitator says: "Begin to disassociate yourself from your fantasy. When you feel ready rejoin the group for processing."

Suggestions for Facilitator Process

Concentrate on the following during processing:

a. What situation did you recall for your hurt? How did you express your feelings? What were you aware of during this time?

b. What did you see when you fantasized about the most beautiful day of your life? What was your body saying to you as you experienced your "day"? How did you express the joy you felt?

*FANTASTIC VOYAGE

Administrative Procedure

a. The facilitator makes the following statement: "I would like you to spread out, lie down, and close your eyes. Try to achieve a comfortable position. Let your body relax and breathe deeply."

b. After sufficient time has elapsed to allow members to reach a point of relaxation, the following instructions are given: "I want you to fantasize that somewhere within your head is a microscopic submarine. You may wish to place it within your mouth, ear, behind your eye or inside your brain. The submarine is so small that it passes easily through your veins. After you've placed your submarine within you I want you to let it flow through your body."

   c. After several minutes the facilitator adds: "Try to get inside your submarine. Look outside its windows at your own body. You now have complete navigational control over your vessel. You may guide it through and within any part or parts of your body. You will be given thirty minutes to make your journey. As you travel, be aware of what you see, feel, sense, etc. Try to explore your *whole* body. Try to discover *all* its feelings. Have a good voyage."

   d. After thirty minutes, or when the facilitator senses the group members have completed their voyages, the processing stage begins.

Suggestions for Facilitator Process

Concentrate on the following during processing:

   a. Where did you originally place your submarine? Why? What did your vessel look like? Where did you go? What did you see, feel, and sense? Did any parts of your body surprise you? Which parts and why?

   b. Where in your body did you stop? How did you feel about the experience? Did you feel you had control of your submarine? Could you actually feel the movement of the submarine?

   c. Have you become more aware of your body? Were there any parts of your body you intentionally stayed away from? If so, what parts and why?

Variations

*Variation I

   a. In order to make the submarine voyage comparable, the facilitator tells *all* members to start the journey from their brain.

   b. He then conducts the journey, having the submarine travel throughout the *entire* body.

   c. The sequence for the journey is at the discretion of the facilitator. He may, however, wish to make sure that the following body parts and areas are covered:

1. brain	11. breasts
2. ears	12. stomach
3. eyes	13. genital area
4. nose	14. buttocks
5. tongue	15. thighs
6. neck	16. knees
7. shoulders	17. ankles
8. chest	18. each toe
9. heart	19. sole of foot
10. lungs	20. heel of foot

*FREE FALL

Administrative Procedure

a. The facilitator says: "Lay down on your back. Close your eyes. Relax. Breathe evenly and deeply."

b. When all appear to be relaxed and at ease, he continues: "Fantasize that you are in an airplane. We are taking off. You have a parachute on. When we reach 20,000 feet, you are going to do a parachute jump and free fall."

c. He continues: "We are slowly climbing. We are at 10,000 feet. Now we are at 15,000 feet. We are now leveling off at 20,000 feet.
I am opening the door. Feel the wind as it enters the plane. Look inside yourself. How do you feel?"

d. He says: "You are now standing at the door. When I say "go," you are to jump. I will call off the height. Feel your sensations and gut level reactions as you free fall. *Whenever* you feel ready, pull your rip cord."
"Jump!"

e. He immediately says: "Feel the wind as it slaps at you and tosses you about.
You are now falling. Spread your arms and legs and free fall. You are now at 15,000 feet.
Now, you are at 12,000 feet. Your body is falling faster.
You are at 9,000 feet. The air is whistling in your ears.
You are at 6,000 feet. The ground seems to be hurtling up to meet you.

You are at 3,000 feet. The ground looks so close you could touch it.

You are at 1,500 feet. You are falling so fast that everything is a blur.

You are now on the ground, falling over as the wind whips your chute. Reel in your parachute. Relax.

Take a few minutes to absorb the experience. We will then discuss it."

Suggestions for Facilitator Process

Concentrate on the following during processing:

a. What feelings did you have during the plane ride, During the free fall? Did you ever feel fear? If so, when? Why? How did you cope with it?
b. Were you able to fantasize yourself free falling? If not, why not? If so, how did it feel?
c. When did you pull your rip cord? Why? How did it feel to land? What have you learned about yourself?

GOOD VIBRATIONS

Administrative Procedure

a. The facilitator says: "Lie down, face up, on the floor. Close your eyes.
b. He then says: "Hum softly. As you hum let the vibrations of the humming flow from your head to your toes."
c. After a few minutes, he says: "Vary the intensity of the humming. Hum loudly, then softly, then keep varying the pitch of your hum. As you do this, pay close attention to the the effects the varied hums have on your body, feelings and reactions."
d. After ten minutes, the facilitator says: "Stop humming. Begin to fantasize that your body is a conglomerate of a million and one vibrations. Try to exercise and move your body as if it were pure energy."
e. After three or four minutes, the facilitator continues:

"Slowly drain the energy and vibrations from your body. After you have done this, breathe evenly and deeply. Try to relax your body. As you are relaxing, try to absorb your experience. When you feel ready, join me. When we are all together, we will discuss this experience."

Suggestions for Facilitator Process

Concentrate on the following during processing:

a. Did you experience your body in a new manner? If so, what did you discover about your body? What effect did the humming have on your body? Did any section(s) of your body have special significance for you? If so, which section(s) and in what way?

b. When fantasizing about your body as one large mass of energy, what were your feelings? Did you move your body? If so, how? If not, why not? What have you learned about your body?

*LAST MINUTES

Administrative Procedure

a. The facilitator makes the following statement: "I would like each one of you to put on a blindfold. We are on a ship that is slowly sinking. We only have thirty minutes of air left. It is inevitable we shall all die, for there is no way out of the ship. When I turn out the lights I want you to become aware of how you will spend your last thirty minutes of life." Lights are turned out.

b. The facilitator adds: "You may move about, talk, touch, hold each other, etc. However, we will spend the last ten minutes in silence."

c. After twenty minutes, the facilitator asks that the remainder of the time be non-verbal.

d. After ten minutes, he says: "We are all dead, get in touch with how you feel. When you are ready, remove your blindfold and slowly come back to life."

e. When all members are ready, processing begins.

Suggestions for Facilitator Process

Concentrate on the following during processing:

a. What did you try to convey to other members during the experience? Did you do or say anything which you normally would not have? What and why? How did you feel about dying?

b. What were you aware of as the time elapsed? Did your mood change when I asked for no talking? What have you gained from this experience?

LETTING GO

Administrative Procedure

a. The facilitator says: "Close your eyes and allow any visions you wish to enter your mind." The members should be given a minimum of five minutes to allow the process to occur.

b. The facilitator then asks the members to let their images flow. He says: "Don't try to 'hold' or 'direct' them. Let them flow."

c. After a few minutes he asks them to physically move their bodies as the images dictate (i.e. head movement, arm movement, facial expressions, etc.).

d. After ten minutes, the members are asked to "erase" their images and concentrate on their body. The facilitator asks members to pay special attention to their stomach, back, legs and neck.

e. After five minutes, the members discuss the experience.

Suggestions for Facilitator Process

Concentrate on the following during processing:

a. What images did you see? Was it difficult to let your mind flow without directing specific thoughts? Did your images have special meaning for you? If so, what was their significance for you?

b. How did you react when asked to physically move with your images? Did you find it added or distracted from your own process of visualization? In what ways did you move?

c. When you became aware of your body were you surprised at what you discovered? Which section of your body felt the most relaxed? The most tense?

LISTENING

Administrative Procedure

a. The facilitator asks members to spread out within the room and assume a comfortable position. He then gives the following instructions: "I want you to lie back and relax. Let your forehead and facial muscles go limp. Let your chest expand and withdraw while letting your arms, hands and stomach untighten. Next, let the floor absorb the weight of your legs, feet, and entire body. I would like you to remain silent and let your mind go blank."

b. After several minutes the facilitator tells the members the following: "Keep your eyes closed. I now want you to cup your hands over your ears and try to block out all sound. I want you to listen to your body, your breathing, your heartbeat, even your pulse. When you are able to "hear" the sounds of your body, try to "feel" yourself. Let your mind wander and try to get in touch with your own being. Images may come to your mind. Try to free yourself from thought and premeditation and let the images occur spontaneously."

c. After ten to fifteen minutes the facilitator asks members to slowly disassociate themselves from the experience and then rejoin the group for processing.

Suggestions for Facilitator Process

Concentrate on the following during processing:

a. What types of sounds did you get in touch with? Did you become aware of parts of your body that you were never aware of before? If so, what were they?

b. What type of images came to your mind? How did you "see" yourself? Did you have any feelings of isolation or separation from yourself? If so, where?

*PRENATAL POSITION

Administrative Procedure

  a. The facilitator says: "Let's take the opportunity to be re-born.
Lie on the floor. Relax. Breathe evenly and deeply."

  b. After a few minutes, he says: "Assume the fetal position. Curl up into a tight ball. You are now a fetus.
You will have fifteen minutes to experience yourself as a fetus growing toward birth. Be aware of your growth. Concentrate on your awakening and expanding awareness."

  c. After fifteen minutes, he says: "It is time to be born. Come out of the womb and enter the world.

Do whatever you feel. Kick, struggle, wiggle, scream or cry. Come into the world. Come out of the womb."

  d. When all members have finished birth, they discuss the experience.

Suggestions for Facilitator Process

Concentrate on the following during processing:

  a. Tell us about your fifteen minute gestation experience. How did you feel? What were you aware of?

  b. Tell us about your birth. Investigate why some fought, some screamed, some came into the world peacefully, etc.

  c. What were your feelings and reactions to birth? What were your feelings and reactions to the entire experience?

PUTTY

Administrative Procedure

  a. The facilitator gives the following introduction: "I have a very large piece of imaginary silly putty. The putty can be shaped, molded, bounced and stretched to form anything we like. I am going to begin by molding my piece of putty and I will then pass it on to the member on my left to be re-shaped in anyway he wishes."

  b. After the facilitator has demonstrated the technique of

        shaping the imaginary putty, he passes it to the member on his left.

  c. After all members have had an opportunity to create with the putty, the facilitator gives the following instructions: "I now want you to imagine that in the center of our circle is a hundred pound piece of putty. I would like us all to start shaping the putty at the same time and create as we go along. This is to be done non-verbally."

  d. After the group has shaped the fantasy putty, the members discuss the experience.

Suggestions for Facilitator Process

Concentrate on the following during processing:

  a. Could you actually feel the putty? If not, why not? What type of sensations did you have? What were your feelings about reshaping another member's creation? What did you create? What meaning does your creation have for you?

  b. How did working on the putty individually differ from working on it as a group? What do you think we ended up with? Were you self-conscious during any part of the exercise? If so, when and why?

STATUES

Administrative Procedure

  a. The facilitator asks members to mill around and non-verbally form dyads.

  b. He then gives the following directions: "I would like you and your partner to face one another. The shorter partner is to try and become as aware as possible of the way in which the taller partner is standing. Without speaking the shorter member is to begin to gently change his partner's posture and facial expression to exaggerate whatever he is most aware of. For example if you are aware of a faint smile you may wish to gently mold your partner's face into a very large smile. Use your hand as if you were molding a piece of clay. Please begin."

c. When each dyad is through with this molding phase, the facilitator says: "I now want the member who did the molding to step back and imitate what he sees before him."
d. Roles are reversed and the same process is repeated.
e. The members then discuss the experience.

Suggestions for Facilitator Process

Concentrate on the following during processing:

a. *To the members being molded:* How did you feel about being touched? Were you able to let yourself be physically manipulated? If not, why not? How did you feel about the position you were being molded into?
b. *To the members molding:* What did you see when you stepped back to look at your creation? Did you find it difficult to imitate the member in front of you? If so, why? Were you aware of your partner's non-verbal cues? What were they? What have you gained from this experience.

*STORIES

Administrative Procedure

a. The facilitator says: "Make up and then write a story about our group that could take place at some future time and place. You will have thirty minutes."
b. After thirty minutes the stories are handed to the facilitator, shuffled, and passed to members to be read aloud. If the member wishes, no name need be attached to the story. No member should read his own story.
c. After all stories have been read, the members discuss the experience.

Suggestions for Facilitator Process

Concentrate on the following during processing:

a. Were you surprised at the content of any of the stories? Which ones? Why? Did you find it difficult to write your story? If so, why? What type of endings seemed to be most common?
b. What type of feelings were expressed most often in the

stories? What insights about the group have you gained from this experience?

SWINGING

Administrative Procedure

a. The facilitator asks the members to close their eyes and imagine a situation in which they feel warm, secure and happy.

b. After a few minutes, he asks the members to open their eyes, look around at the other members and silently compare what they are now seeing and feeling with what they saw and felt during their fantasy.

c. The facilitator repeats steps *a* and *b*.

d. The members then discuss the experience.

Suggestions for Facilitator Process

Concentrate on the following during processing:

a. How did it feel to go back and forth between the "here and now" and the "there and then"? What type of fantasies did you have when your eyes were closed? What did you see and feel? How does that situation differ from the situation encountered when you opened your eyes?

b. What types of feelings did you have when you looked around at the other members? What have you learned about yourself? Was there any change in your fantasy when you repeated the process? If so in what way? How do you explain this?

*TABOO FANTASY

Administrative Procedure

a. The facilitator asks that each member find a private corner in the room and then lie down, face up, with their eyes closed.

b. The facilitator may then wish to give a brief talk on the value of having sexual fantasises without feeling guilt-ridden.

c. Members are then asked to fantasize about their sexual feelings, whether they be toward another member or members in the group or toward someone else.

d. After several minutes the group rejoins and volunteers are sought who are willing to share their sexual fantasies with the group.

e. When all who wish to relate their fantasies have had the opportunity to do so, processing begins.

Suggestions for Facilitator Process

Concentrate on the following during processing:

a. *To all members:* How did you feel about being asked to fantasize sexually? Did you experience any fear or guilt? If so how did you handle it?

b. *To those who volunteered:* What type of reaction do you feel the group gave you when you shared your fantasy? What went through your mind when I asked you to volunteer? How do you feel toward the group?

*TO THE BOTTOM OF THE SEA

Administrative Procedure

a. The facilitator says: "Let's take the opportunity to let our imaginations run wild. We are going to become aquanauts and swim to the bottom of the sea.

First, lie back and relax. Begin to fantasize that you are an aquanaut."

b. After several minutes, he continues: "We are on a boat in the middle of the ocean. The boat is gently rocking as the waves slap against it. Feel the motion.

When I say go, jump over the side. Be aware of your body hitting the water and becoming one with it.
Go."

c. After a few seconds, he says: "Swim toward the bottom. It's a long, long way down. As you swim, be aware of the beauty you are encountering. Be aware of your feelings and reactions to the sea environment and the life it holds.

Swim slowly, relax and enjoy what you are doing."

d. After three or four minutes, the facilitator says: "You are now at the bottom of the sea. You are going to encounter a sea denizen, one which will terrify you.

  There it is. See it. Feel your reactions. Be aware of your body and what it is saying to you."

e. After two minutes, he says: "The terrifying animal is swimming away. Be aware of how you now feel, knowing that it is gone."

f. After a minute, he continues: "Here comes a sea denizen which fills you with joy, elation and peace. It is so beautiful and meaningful to you. Be aware of your feelings. Enjoy them."

g. After three or four minutes, the facilitator says: "Say goodbye to your beautiful friend and slowly swim back to the boat.
  When we are all ready, we will discuss this experience."

Suggestions for Facilitator Process

Concentrate on the following during processing:

a. How did you feel prior to jumping into the water? How did you feel during your swim to the bottom? What did you see?

b. What terrifying creature did you encounter? Investigate why some members met real creatures (sharks, sting rays, etc.), while others invented creatures. How did you feel during the encounter with this sea animal?

c. What beautiful sea animal did you encounter? Again investigate the reasons for encountering real or imaginary creatures. How did you feel in the presence of this animal? How do you feel now? What have you learned about yourself?

Variations

*Variation I

a. To make the swim *entirely* pleasureable, repeat the original fantasy with the following exceptions:

1. Delete steps *d* and *e*.
2. Concentrate heavily in all other stages on the peace, beauty and tranquility being encountered.

WATERFALL

Administrative Procedure

a. The facilitator asks members to spread out, find a spot in the room, and assume a comfortable position. He then says: "Close your eyes. Try to relax as much as possible. Let your muscles relax and your tensions flow out."

b. The following instructions are given: "I want you to imagine that you are a waterfall in the mountains. Try and *become* this waterfall, get in touch with its movement and texture."

c. After several minutes the facilitator adds: "Near the waterfall is a large tree. I now want you to *be* this tree. Concentrate on your shape, size, etc."

d. After enough time has elapsed for members to become involved in their fantasies, the facilitator concludes by saying: "As the tree I want you to look at the waterfall and say goodbye. When you have fully absorbed the experience, I want you to open your eyes."

e. The members then discuss the experience.

Suggestions for Facilitator Process

Concentrate on the following during processing:

a. What feelings did you have during your fantasies? Did you find it difficult to relax and let the images flow spontaneously? Will you share with the group a description of your waterfall?

b. What type of tree did you become? What types of objects did you see as a tree? How did you feel looking at the waterfall? How did you say goodbye to it?

c. Which of the two fantasies was most enjoyable? Why? Which was most difficult to get into? Why? What have you learned about yourself?

Variations

*Variation I

a. Steps *a* and *b* of the original exercise are repeated.

b. The facilitator then says: "Near the river at the top of the waterfall is a tree. Be that tree. Feel its texture. Imagine its size and coloring."

c. After a few minutes, he says: "You, the tree, are falling into the river. Feel yourself falling. Feel the water as you strike it."

d. After a moment, he continues: "You, the tree, are drifting toward the falls. Feel the journey. As you go over the edge, feel the tree's feelings. Think the tree's thoughts. Be aware of the tree's feelings and sensations as it strikes the water at the bottom of the falls."

e. After three or four minutes, the facilitator says: "Slowly come out of your fantasy. Become yourself. When you are ready, we will discuss this experience."

f. During processing, concentrate on the types of feelings the tree had during its journey. Did it feel fear or did it feel comfortable and protected by the river? Did the falls destroy it or cushion its fall? Were there rocks at the bottom of the falls? Such questions and their answers give considerable insight into the fear, hope, desires, stereotyping behavior, etc. of the members.

*WESTERN TOWN

Administrative Procedure

a. The facilitator asks members to close their eyes and try to imagine becoming a character in a Western Town. The facilitator may wish to suggest a number of roles to choose from e.g. town drunk, saloon girl, sheriff, good citizen, small boy, judge, outlaw, horse, etc.

b. He then adds: "When I ask you to open your eyes I want you to act out your role without speaking. You may only interact with the other members on a non-verbal level. I want to encourage you to act out your character as freely and as uninhibitedly as possible. You may make use of the entire room."

c. After the facilitator feels the scene has been acted out to its full potential, the group rejoins and the following instructions are given: "I would now like you to verbally give each member a new "Western Town" role. Feel free to give your rationale for assigning the new role to the member in question. If a number of roles are given to one member he may choose from among those roles the one he most highly identifies with."

d. After each member has been assigned a new role, step *b* is repeated. The role enactments, however, are now verbal.

e. After the scene has been acted out, the facilitator says: "Close you eyes. Think of a name for our "Western Town." Try to make the name relevant and meaningful to yourself and/or our group."

f. The facilitator, after a few moments, has the members share their town names. They are encouraged to give the rationale for the relevancy of their names.

g. The facilitator then says: "Mill around non-verbally. You have ten minutes to decide which member's town name we will adopt for our Western Town."

h. The members then discuss the experience.

Suggestions for Facilitator Process

Concentrate on the following during processing:

a. What role did you originally assign yourself? How did you act out that role? In what way did you non-verbally interact with the other members? Did you *become* your role?

b. How did you feel about the role(s) assigned to you? Which role did you feel more comfortable with, the one you gave yourself or the one given to you? How did your behavior during the second role interaction differ from the first interaction?

c. Did you feel that any type of story developed from the group's interaction? What have you learned about the other members in the group? About yourself?

    d. Whose town name did we choose? Why? If consensus was not reached, ask why. What did we learn about each other as a result of the name development?

Variations

Variation I-V

    a. Instead of a western town setting, the facilitator may create a setting more suitable to the needs of himself or the group. Following are some suggested locales:

        I. A space ship.

        II. A party where famous people are gathered.

        III. A cartoon strip made up of present day cartoon characters.

        IV. A city from the time of the Roman Empire.

        V. The personnel at an Air Force base.

*Variations VI-VII

    a. The facilitator explains the concept of the Western Town.

    b. He then says that any member who wishes a locale fantasized should feel free to state the locale.

    c. If more than one locale is suggested, the group can (VI) reach a non-verbal consensus as to which *one* locale will be explored, or (VII) fantasize about each locale, one at a time.

III

FEEDBACK

THE PRIMARY GOAL for each exercise in this chapter is the elicitation of feedback material.

Feedback is an essential dynamic in all groups, especially for encounter, personal growth, marathon and t-groups. It is generally received at a verbal level. However, the facilitator must recognize that members frequently find out where they are with others through non-verbal means. Because non-verbal means of communicating feedback are so rampant during the group session, it would seem wise for the facilitator to take advantage of them by utilizing a non-verbal feedback exercise.

Members should learn about the ways in which feedback is received and transmitted non-verbally. The exercises in this chapter offer them these opportunities.

It is important for the facilitator to remember that these exercises elicit non-verbal forms of feedback. We impress upon him this fact because there is *always* the possibility that non-verbal feedback will be either miscommunicated or improperly received. Because of this, the processing stage becomes enormously important. The facilitator *must* use the processing stage to insure that the feedback given was received and interpreted accurately.

*BACK TALK

Subsidiary Goal(s)
    a. To explore that dynamics of non-verbal communication.
    b. To gain greater awareness of one's own body.

Group Application
    Twelve members or less. Since dyads are used, group size should be even. To be used with encounter, personal growth, marathon and t-groups.

Application Variables

Fifteen minutes. The exercise is 100 per cent non-verbal. The room should be large enough to allow dyads to spread out unrestrained.

Administrative Procedure

a. The facilitator asks the members to form dyads and to then find an area within the room where they feel some degree of privacy.
b. He then tells the dyadic partners to sit with their backs to one another and to close their eyes.
c. The facilitator instructs the dyads: "Say hello to your partner using only your back. Try to get to know your partner's back, communicate with your partner. Tell him how your back feels."
d. After a few minutes the facilitator says: "Using only your back, communicate with your partner. Tell him how you feel about him at this moment."
e. After five minutes members are told to lock arms and stand up.
f. When the dyads are standing, the facilitator continues: "Release your arms and say goodbye. Using your back only."
g. The members then discuss the experience.

Suggestions for Facilitator Process

Concentrate on the following during processing:

a. What did your partner non-verbally say to you? Were you surprised at any of the messages you perceived? Which ones and why? How did you say hello? Do you feel you really got to know your partner's back?
b. What did you discover about your own back? Was it difficult saying goodbye? If so, why? Did you feel mutual support when helping one another stand?

Variations

None

Figure 3-1. Back Talk

Figure 3-2. Back Talk

FACES

Subsidiary Goal(s)

    a. To explore the dynamics involved in creativity.

    b. To examine members' feelings and attitudes towards themselves and others.

    c. To become in touch with facial expressions.

Group Application

    Twelve members or less. To be used with encounter, personal growth, marathon and t-groups.

Application Variables

    Fifteen minutes. The exercise is 100 per cent non-verbal. The room must be large enough to allow two sub-groups of 5 to 7 members to be comfortably seated.

Administrative Procedure

    a. The facilitator asks the large group to form two subgroups consisting of 5 to 7 members.

    b. The two subgroups are to be seated comfortably in circles.

    c. The facilitator gives the following instructions: "I want one of you to begin by creating a facial expression. After one of you has done this turn to your left and allow the member on your left to copy your facial expression. The member copying your facial expression is to hold if for a few seconds. He then turns his head toward the left. Before he reaches the next person on his left the member is to non-verbally create a new facial expression for the next member to copy. Don't plan your expressions but rather let them occur spontaneously."

    d. The above process is repeated until all members in the circle have participated.

    e. The facilitator then asks the members to close their eyes and quietly absorb the experience.

Suggestions for Facilitator Process

    Concentrate on the following during processing:

    a. What did your facial expressions represent? Was it difficult copying a member's facial expression? If so why?

b. What were the other members' facial expressions like? Was it difficult to spontaneously create your own? What type of feeling do you have about the experience? What have you learned about the other members in your subgroup?

Variations

None

*FAMILY TREE

Subsidiary Goal(s)

a. To explore the dynamics involved in fantasy.
b. To examine member relationships.
c. To increase awareness.

Group Application

Twelve members or less. To be used with encounter, personal growth, marathon and t-groups. Best results are obtained if the exercise is used late in the group's life.

Application Variables

One hour. The exercise is 100 per cent non-verbal. Written activity occupies 25 per cent of the non-verbal activity. Pencils, paper and an overhead projector are required. If a projection machine is not available, mimeographs of each paper may be used.

Administrative Procedure

a. The facilitator asks each member to create a family tree using members in the group. If the group meets on a daily or weekly basis, it is suggested that the members do this in between sessions.
b. The following formats are suggested as possible methods for describing the family relationships.

I.

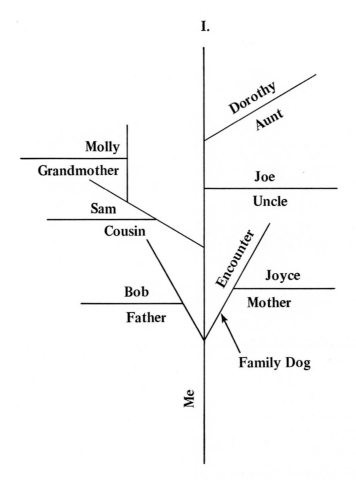

Figure 3-3. Family Tree

II.

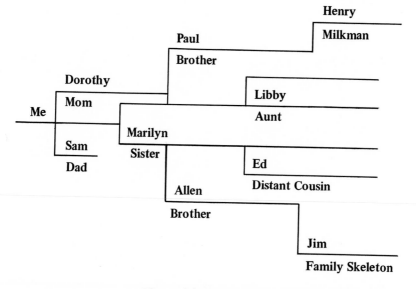

Figure 3-4. Family Tree

III.

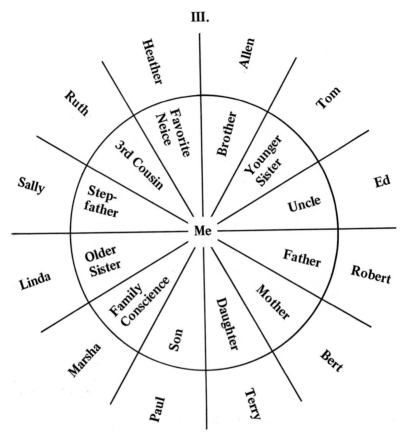

Figure 3-5. Family Tree

c. The family trees are then reproduced for the entire group via projection or mimeograph.
d. The members should be given thirty to forty-five minutes to non-verbally study all the family trees.
e. The group then discusses the family trees and the entire experience.

Suggestions for Facilitator Process

Concentrate on the following during processing:

a. Were you surprised at your position on the family tree?

Whose tree? Why were you surprised? Were you placed consistently in one role? Which one? How do you explain this?
How did you feel about the roles you were assigned?

b. What have you learned about other members' perceptions of
you? Do you feel that the group is a family? Were you surprised at other members' placement of themselves?

Variations

None

*FEELING FEEDBACK

Subsidiary Goal(s)

a. To learn to non-verbally express positive and negative feelings.

b. To learn how one copes with giving and receiving positive
and negative feedback.

Group Application

Twelve members or less. To be used with encounter, personal
growth, marathon and t-groups whose members have developed
feelings of warmth, care, and trust for each other.

Application Variables

Time is dependent upon the number of members who volunteer to receive feedback. Usually, each member volunteering
will use five to ten minutes. The exercise is 100 per cent non-
verbal.

Administrative Procedure

a. The facilitator says: "We have learned how to give and receive verbal feedback. However, we have done little in the
area of non-verbally giving and receiving feedback. Can I
have a volunteer who will help us investigate this process?"

b. The facilitator has the volunteer stand in the center of the
group circle. He tells him: "Close your eyes. We will be
giving you feedback as to how we feel toward you. You are
not to return it.

c. The facilitator then tells the other members: "One at a time, in whatever order you wish, go to (name the volunteer) and express non-verbally the negative feelings you have for him."

d. When this is finished, the facilitator says: "Now, go and express non-verbally the positive feelings you have for him."

e. When this is completed, the facilitator may process or ask for another volunteer. We recommend *immediate* processing. This insures that the volunteer will be attended to *before* he has the opportunity to forget feelings.

f. The post-feedback processing suggested should concentrate on the volunteer's feelings and reactions, on the messages sent and received, on the manner in which they were transmitted, on the accuracy and inaccuracy of the volunteer's interpretations, and on which type of feedback was most meaningful to the volunteer and why it was most meaningful.

g. The exercise continues until all who wish the feeling feedback experience have had the opportunity to do so.

Suggestions for Facilitator Process

Concentrate on the following during processing:

a. *To all volunteers:* What were your feelings during each feedback phase? Which feedback was most meaningful to you? Why? How did it feel to be unable to return feelings? How did you cope with these feelings? How did it feel not knowing who gave you the feedback? How did you cope with these feelings?

b. *To all:* What feelings were you transmitting? How did you convey them? Which feelings, positive or negative, were easiest to convey? Why? Why was it so difficult expressing the other type of feelings?

Variations

*Variation I

a. Whenever the facilitator notices that a member expresses a negative self-concept and is continually downgrading himself, he asks the member to enter the center of the circle.

b. He then repeats the directions found in step *b* of the original exercise.

c. He then has the group express *only* positive feelings they have for the member.

d. Proceessing should center on the fact that the member *is* loved and cared for. This will help him start to develop some positive feelings for himself.

*Variation II

a. Whenever the facilitator notices that a member is too positive about himself, he asks the member to enter the center of the circle.

b. He then repeats the directions found in step *b* of the original exercise.

c. He then has the group express *only* negative feelings they have for the member.

d. Processing should center on the fact that the member is *not* perceived by others as perfect. This will help him start to more honestly evaluate himself as a person who affects other individuals both positively *and* negatively.

*IMITATIONS

Subsidiary Goal(s)

a. To learn to communicate non-verbally.

b. To learn to non-verbally unload hidden agendas.

c. To learn the place projection plays in non-verbally indicating how we perceive others.

Group Application

Twelve members or less. To be used only with encounter, personal growth, marathon and t-groups whose members have developed warmth, care, and trust for each other.

Application Variables

Time is unlimited and is dependent upon the number of dyads who "imitate" each other. Dyads involved will use approximately ten to fifteen minutes per imitation sequence.

Administrative Procedure

a. Whenever the facilitator notices that two members are experiencing negative feelings for each other, are not communicating, or appear to have hidden agendas between them, he asks that they enter the center of the circle and stand facing each other.

b. He tells the dyad: "I, and others, have noticed the communication problems you are having with each other. Since you appear unable or unwilling to overcome them verbally, let's enter into a non-verbal exercise. Maybe you can overcome them through this method.

   Decide who will go first. The individual who goes first is to imitate those aspects of his partner which are behind his negative reactions. The observing partner is to watch as *he* is imitated. He is not to react!"

c. He tells the observers to study the non-verbal communication which occurs and to be ready to give the dyad feedback.

d. When it becomes apparent that the imitator is finished, the facilitator says to the imitator: "Turn your back to your partner."

e. He then tells the partner to react non-verbally to the imitation of himself he observed. He says: "React as you feel. React in accordance to what you believe the imitator was telling you about yourself."

f. When this is completed, the facilitator tells the imitator: "Face your partner. Now, be him. React as *you* believe he would react to your imitation of him."

g. When this is finished, the dyad and the observers process the imitation. See the Suggestions for Facilitator Process section.

h. The partners are then allowed to reverse roles and the exercise is repeated. Processing *must* investigate the extent to which the second member's imitation was influenced by the first partner's miming of him.

i. Any other members who wish to experience the exercise should be given the opportunity to do so.

Suggestions for Facilitator Process

Concentrate on the following during processing:

a. *To imitated member:* What was your partner telling you about yourself? How did you feel about this? Why do you feel your reaction differed from his predicted reaction? Have your feelings toward him changed? If so, how and why? If not, why not?

b. *To the imitator:* What were you telling your partner? Do you feel he "got the message." If no, why not? Have your feelings toward him changed? If so, how and why? If not, why not?

c. *To the observers:* Tell the imitator what behavior he exhibited which struck you as being meaningful. Do the same for the receiving member. Tell the imitator what he did which made you believe he was projecting his own feelings on his partner.

Variations

None

*LIBRARY

Subsidiary Goal(s)

a. To explore the dynamics involved in fantasy.
b. To gain greater awareness of members' perceptions.
c. To explore the process of creativity.

Group Application

Twelve members or less. To be used only with encounter, personal growth, marathon and t-groups.

Application Variables

Forty-five minutes. The exercise is 50 per cent non-verbal and 50 per cent verbal. Three by five notecards (equal to the group size squared) and pencils are required. For example, a twelve member group requires 144 cards.

Administrative Procedure

a. The facilitator passes out three by five notecards to each member (including himself) equal to the number of members in the group and gives the following introduction: "Pretend that we are all books in a library. As you know, a library contains books on thousands of topics and subjects. These range from mystery novels to scientific journals. For each member in the group fill out one three by five card with the type of book or magazine which most accurately describes your impression of that member. Make out one for yourself as well. Place the members name you are describing on the back of the card."

b. After all members have completed the card filling process, the facilitator states: "Please pass all cards to me except for the one you filled out on yourself. I will sort them out according to individual members. I will then read the cards. As soon as you feel that one set of cards describes you, claim those cards. If two members claim the same packet of cards, you must decide between you who they belong to. I will read them all once and go back and read them again. After you have claimed a packet of cards they will be given to you. Do not look at the back of the cards to find out if you were right until all cards have been passed out."

c. After all cards have been claimed, one member at a time is to reveal his own card as well as who the packet of cards he claimed belong to, be it himself or some other member.

d. The group members then discuss the experience.

Suggestions for Facilitator Process

Concentrate on the following during processing:

a. What type of feedback did you receive? If you chose the wrong cards how did you feel? Do you perceive yourself as being similar to the member they were intended for? If so, in what way? If not, how do you explain your wrong choice?

b. Were you surprised at any of the feedback you received? If so, which and why? What insights have you gained about yourself? About others?

Variations

None

*LEAVES, FLOWERS, BUGS AND THINGS

Subsidiary Goal(s)

a. To become more in touch with nature.
b. To gain insight into members' perceptions.
c. To heighten the sharing experience.

Group Application

Twelve members or less. To be used with encounter, personal growth, marathon and t-groups. The exercise is designed to be used after members have had ample time to form impressions of other members.

Application Variables

Thirty minutes to one hour. The exercise is 100 per cent non-verbal. Since the exercise is to take place outside, the group must have access to a large and open outdoor area in which trees and leaves are abundant.

Administrative Procedure

a. The facilitator makes the following statement: "We will have the next thirty to forty-five minutes to walk around alone. As you are walking, I want you to gather one object for every member including yourself which represents your feelings and impressions toward that member. Please feel free to let your imagination and creativity run wild. I will call out when the time has elapsed. Please begin."

b. After all members have come back to the original spot, the facilitator states: "Without speaking or asking any questions or giving any explanations, give your objects to the appropriate members. This means that each member should receive one object from you and you should have been given one object by each member."

c. After all members have given and received their objects,

they are given time to examine them.

d. After several minutes, the members discuss the experience.

Suggestions for Facilitator Process

Concentrate on the following during processing:

a. What type of objects did you receive? Did you give? Do you feel you received consistent feedback? If so, what are people saying to you? Which object do you appreciate the most? Why? Which object's meaning are you most unsure of? Why?

b. How close did you feel with nature while going on your walk? What were you aware of? What role did your creativity and imagination play in your selections? What insights have you gained?

c. Members should be given an opportunity to check out their interpretations of the object received with various members after processing. This allows for an unbiased appraisal by the receiving members.

Variations

None

*LOGS

Subsidiary Goal(s)

a. To give and receive feedback.

b. To allow members to sort through intense emotional experiences.

c. To explore the dynamics involved in the use of writing as a communication process.

Group Application

Any number of members. To be used with any group meeting over a period of time. Best results are obtained if the exercise is used throughout the group's life, beginning with the first session.

Application Variables

One hour. The exercise is 100 per cent non-verbal. Pencils and paper are required. The exercise is done outside the group, although processing may occur within the group setting.

Administrative Procedure

a. The facilitator, at the first session, asks the members to write a log for each session.

b. It may be helpful if the facilitator gives a brief talk on the value of sorting out intense experiences and the importance of written communication.

c. The members are told that the logs should be approximately one page in length. They can use any format similar to the example given after the *Variations* section of this exercise.

d. The members should be instructed to wait a few hours or even a day before attempting to write their logs. This period of time allows the member to look at his experiences and investigate them more congruently.

e. Before the beginning of each session the logs of the last session are passed around. Comments and feedback may be given at that time.

Suggestions for Facilitator Process

Concentrate on the following during processing:

a. Do you feel there is any unfinished business? Did anyone's log surprise you? How did you sort through your own experiences?

b. Was it difficult to differentiate between thoughts and feelings? What have you discovered about yourself?

Variations

Variation I

a. The format of the log may be expanded to include poetry, paintings, etc.

GROUP LOG EXAMPLE

Name_____

Date_____

Session_____

Incident	*Feelings*	*Thoughts*
A. Confrontation between Ken and I.	A. Awkwardness, anger, hurt.	A. I think I was being defensive.
B. Sexual discussion with Linda.	B. Risk, arousal, confusion.	B. I wish she would let me love her.
C. Not disclosing what I felt toward Judy.	C. Disappointment in myself.	C. She wouldn't have been able to handle it.
	D. Afraid I would be rejected.	D. It doesn't really matter.

*OBJECTS #1

Subsidiary Goal(s)

a. To gain greater insight into members' self-concepts.

b. To further enhance member relationships.

c. To develop insight into symbolism.

Group Application

Twelve members or less. To be used with encounter, personal growth, marathon and t-groups.

Application Variables

One hour. The exercise is 50 per cent non-verbal and 50 per cent verbal.

Administrative Procedure

a. At the end of the session the facilitator asks that each member bring to the next session an object which symbolically represents himself and one object for each member which symbolically represents them. (If the exercise is used in a marathon group, the members should be given one hour to locate the objects.) If there are a total of twelve members in the group each member is to bring twelve objects.

b. After the objects have been collected, each member passes out the objects to the appropriate members. He places his own in front of him.

c. The facilitator asks that the members silently study the objects given to them.

d. After fifteen minutes each member is to verbally present the objects he brought for himself and the rationale for bringing that specific object.

e. After all members have presented their own objects, members may pair off into smaller subgroups to discuss the other objects received.

f. After forty-five minutes, the group members discuss the experience.

Suggestions for Facilitator Process

Concentrate on the following during processing:

a. Were you surprised at any of the objects you received? It so why? Do you find any consistency among the items you received? If yes, in what way? How do you explain this?

b. Did you have a difficult time in selecting an object which symbolically represented you? What have you learned about any of the group members that you did not know before?

Variations

None

POETRY

Subsidiary Goal(s)

a. To explore the dynamics involved in creativity.

b. To achieve greater awareness, both introspectively and interpersonally.

c. To experience communication on a written level.

Group Application

Twelve members or less. To be used with encounter, personal growth, marathon and t-groups. With the exception of marathon groups, the exercise is intended to be used between sessions. If this is not feasible, the exercise can be easily adapted to be used during the group's session.

Application Variables

Forty-five minutes to one hour. The exercise is 100 per cent non-verbal. Pencils and paper are required for each member.

Administrative Procedure

a. At the end of the session, the facilitator says: "Often we tend to overlook the artistic value of writing as a valid mode of communication in our everyday lives. I would like you to write a poem dealing with your experiences in the group thus far. It may be as short or as long as you wish. You may deal with your experiences with the entire group, another individual or just yourself. Please bring your poems with you to the next session. They will be read aloud and discussed by the entire group." (If it is impossible for members to write between sessions, forty-five minutes to one hour should be set aside for writing) .

b. At the next session the facilitator asks that the members read their poems. When all members have finished reading their poems, the group discusses them and the experience.

Suggestions for Facilitator Process

Concentrate on the following during processing:

a. What did you experience as you wrote your poetry? Did you gain any new insights? If so, what? How did you feel about having your poetry read to the entire group? Did this prior knowledge affect your writing?

b. Were you surprised at any of the members' poetry? Whose and why? What did you learn about the other members' creative resources? What type of feedback did the group receive? Did you receive?

Variations

None

*RANKING

Subsidiary Goal(s)

a. To gain awareness of members' perceptions.
b. To explore the dynamics involved in confrontation.
c. To gain awareness of non-verbal cues.

Group Application

Twelve members or less. To be used with any group concerned with honest and direct feedback. The facilitator should be aware that intense emotional reaction may be elicited. Therefore, he should use the processing stage to insure that such feelings are resolved.

Application Variables

Forty-five minutes to one hour. The exercise is 100 per cent non-verbal. The room must be large enough to allow members unrestrained movement.

Administrative Procedure

a. The facilitator states: "This exercise is designed to give us an opportunity to engage in direct and frank feedback at a non-verbal level.
We are going to rank ourselves on a variety of criteria. Pretend there is an imaginary straight line down the center of the room. When I give a criteria begin to rank yourselves from most (at the head of the line) to least (at the end of the line)."
b. The following criteria are given one at a time. The facilitator does not proceed to the next criteria until all members have ranked themselves.

   1. influence in the group
   2. sensitivity
   3. honesty
   4. openness
   5. defensiveness
   6. facilitativeness
   7. emotionality

    8. anger
    9. ability to be hurt
  10. competitiveness

The above order is arbitrary. All or part of the criteria may be used as time and appropriateness permit.

c. After ranking is completed, the members discuss the experience.

Suggestions for Facilitator Process

Concentrate on the following during processing:

a. Were you consistently ranking yourself? Why? Did you disagree with any of the rankings? If so, what did you do about it? How did you resolve any conflicts?

b. Were you surprised at any of the rankings? What type of feedback did you receive from this exercise? What have you learned about yourself? About others? How do you feel now about yourself and the group? Ask those with negative feelings what can be done to alleviate those feelings.

Variations

None

SING A SONG

Subsidiary Goal(s)

a. To become more aware of members' perceptions.

b. To explore the dynamics involved in overcoming inhibitions.

c. To gain insight into members' creative processes.

d. To give members an opportunity for constructive play.

Group Application

Twelve members or less. To be used with encounter, personal growth, marathon and t-groups. Best results are obtained if the exercise is used after the group has had ample time to develop a climate of trust and cohesion.

Application Variables

Thirty to forty-five minutes. The exercise is 50 per cent non-verbal and 50 per cent verbal. The room must be large enough to allow each member private space. Pencils and paper are required.

Administrative Procedure

a. The facilitator presents the following introduction: "There are many different ways in which we can give feedback. This exercise is designed to elicit our creative resources when dealing with feedback.

I am going to pass out paper and pencils to each of you. You will have the next twenty minutes to compose a song about the group or the individual members in the group. You may put your lyrics to any melody you wish. Let your imagination run free. When time is up we will rejoin in the large circle and sing our songs to the group. Your song may be as short or as long as you wish. Please begin."

b. After twenty minutes the group rejoins in the large group. The facilitator may wish to make a statement to ease inhibitions about singing in front of others. A volunteer is asked to begin.

c. After each member has had an opportunity to sing his song, the group begins processing.

Suggestions for Facilitator Process

Concentrate on the following during processing:

a. How did you feel about singing in front of others? How did you cope with these feelings? What type of feedback do you feel was most common? Did anyone's song surprise you? If so, whose and why?

b. What process did you go through in creating your song? Did you make up an original melody? If not, why not? What were you aware of while singing? What were you aware of while others were singing? Whose song was most original Why do you say this?

Variations

Variation I
a. Have members spend twenty minutes composing their songs.
b. The songs are then mixed in a pile and given out at random. They are to be sung by the member drawing the lyrics. No member, however, should sing his own song.

IV

GETTING ACQUAINTED

T HE PRIMARY GOAL for each exercise in this chapter is the facilitation of the getting acquainted process.

Getting acquainted is a necessary phase which all groups must go through, regardless of whether members have had past exposure to one another or to the group experience. The exercises in this chapter are designed to provide a structure which is conducive to initiating interaction between members in the hopes that they will get to know each other more rapidly. They also serve as an early introduction to non-verbal means of communication.

Processing is exceedingly important for such exercises for a multitude of reasons. We enumerate some of them. First, processing helps insure that the first impressions formed during the getting acquainted stage do *not* interfere with forthcoming group sessions. It does this by helping the members investigate and clarify such initial impressions. Second, processing helps the members gain greater awareness of, and insight into, their interactions with one another and into the getting acquainted process. Third, it helps the members recognize and cope with their reactions to non-verbal means of communicating. Fourth, it serves as a means of preparing the members to cope with non-verbal exercises which might be used later in the life of the group.

There are other reasons for processing getting acquainted exercises. The four listed above, however, should be sufficient as evidence for exhaustive processing.

*BUMP AND GRIND

Subsidiary Goal(s)

a. To encourage participation.
b. To learn how one feels about touching and being touched.
c. To develop warmth between members.

Group Application

Twenty members or less. Since dyads are used, group size should be even. Applicable to any group, but most frequently used at the first or second session of encounter, personal growth, marathon and t-groups.

Application Variables

Fifteen minutes. The exercise is 100 per cent non-verbal.

Administrative Procedure

a. The facilitator says: "Form a circle with your backs facing inward. Stretch the circle until only your finger tips are touching."

b. He then says: "Close your eyes and move backwards toward each other. When you bump into someone, use your rear end to say hello to him. After you have said hello, find another and do the same. Try to bump hello to as many members as you can."

c. After two or three minutes, he says: "Keeping your eyes closed, find a partner and stand back to back. Do not link arms."

d. When the dyads are formed, the facilitator says: "Using only your rear ends, backs, and shoulders, communicate with each other. Tell your partner how you feel about him. Remember to keep your eyes closed."

e. After three minutes, the facilitator says: "You may now use your head to help the communication."

f. After three minutes, he continues: "Sit down, back-to-back. Using your backs, shoulders and head, give each other back massages."

g. After three minutes, the facilitator says: "Move away from your partner. Concentrate on your rear end, back, head and shoulders. Be aware of how they feel."

h. After a minute, he says: "Turn and look at your partner. Express your feelings for him non-verbally, then we will discuss the exercise."

Suggestions for Facilitator Process

Concentrate on the following during processing:

a. How did you feel at the start of the exercise? How did your feelings change as the exercise progressed? Why did they change?

b. Which of the dyadic phases was most meaningful? Why? Which was most difficult? Why? Which did you enjoy the least? Why?

c. Which dyadic phase was most conducive to communication? Why? What feelings did you send? How? What feelings did you receive?

d. What feelings do you now have toward your partner? Did the exercise contribute to the development of these feelings? If yes, how and why? If no, why not?

Variations

None

*TOUCH AND KNOW

Subsidiary Goal(s)

a. To learn how one feels about touching and being touched.
b. To learn to tune into tactile exploration and sensations.
c. To develop warmth between members.

Group Application

Group size is unlimited. However, if processing is to occur, the size should be twelve members or less. Since dyads are used, group size should be even. Applicable to any group, but most frequently used at the first session of encounter, personal growth, marathon and t-groups.

Application Variables

Ten to fifteen minutes. The exercise is 100 per cent non-verbal. The room should be large enough to allow the group members to mill comfortably.

Administrative Procedure

a. The facilitator says: "We all too frequently rely on facts and words in getting to know another. Before we do that today, let's try to get to know some people non-verbally. Please stand up and move the chairs and furniture out of the way."

b. When this is completed, he says: "Close your eyes. At *no time* are you to open your eyes. Mill around until you find some person you *feel* you would like to know. When you have done this, stand together. When all the dyads are formed, I will give you further instructions. Remember, keep your eyes closed."

c. When the dyads are formed, he continues: "Now, explore your partner's face. Try to visualize the other person. What does he look like? What is he feeling? What *is* he as a person? Do this until I tell you to stop. Do not open your eyes at any time."

d. After three minutes, the facilitator says: "Stop exploring. Keeping your eyes closed, find another partner. When all the dyads are formed I will give you further instructions."

e. When this is done, he says: "With your right hand, explore your own face. With your left hand, explore your partner's face. Try to touch and explore the same spot, object, or area on his face that you are touching and exploring on your own."

f. After a minute, he continues: "What feelings are you having? What feelings do you believe your partner is having? Do you feel a oneness growing between you? Keep touching and exploring."

g. After two minutes, the facilitator tells the members to open their eyes, look at their partner, and return to the original group circle so the experience can be discussed.

Suggestions for Facilitator Process

Concentrate on the following during processing:

a. Look around the circle. Go to the person you believe was your first partner. *To those who were correct:* explain this. *To those who were incorrect:* tell us why you were wrong.

b. Which of the two experiences was most meaningful? Why? Was touching and being touched easier during the second experience than the first? Why? If not, why not?

c. Which of your partners do you feel you know best? Why? What happened with your other partner to impede the knowing process? What did your partners do to make you believe they were gentle, kind, warm, aggressive, hesitant, etc.?

Variations

*Variation I

a. Notice the dyadic match-ups during the first experience.

b. In step *d,* ask that dyads that were mixed i.e. male and female, seek new partners of the *same* sex. That is, male should seek a male, and the female should seek a female.

c. During processing, have the same sex dyads compare their second experience with the first. Have them investigate the dynamics, sexual and otherwise, which affected the second experience.

VISUAL VERSUS NON-VISUAL GROPING AND MILLING

Subsidiary Goal(s)

a. To learn that closing one's eyes can enhance the getting acquainted process.

b. To develop warmth between members.

c. To learn to communicate feelings non-verbally.

d. To learn to interpret feelings communicated to us non-verbally.

e. To learn how one feels about touching and being touched.

Group Application

Twenty members or less. Applicable to any group, but most frequently used at the first session of encounter, personal growth, marathon and t-groups.

Application Variables

Fifteen minutes. The exercise is 100 per cent non-verbal. The room must be large enough to allow the group members to mill comfortably.

Administrative Procedure

a. The facilitator says: "We frequently look at a person and get a feeling that we, somehow, know that person. However, looking can be a hinderance. Let's engage in a non-verbal exercise to prove this.

b. He continues: "Close your eyes and mill about. Grope for other people. When you find someone, non-verbally say hello to him.

After you have greeted him, explore him. Use your fingers and hands to get to know him. Touch his head, face, hair, eyes, and so on. Try to send him a feeling message. Let him know where he is with you. Try also to read the message he is sending you.

When you have completed your touch conversation, say good-bye non-verbally. You should then mill and grope until you find another partner. Keep your eyes closed at *all* times. Continue until I tell you to stop."

c. After ten minutes, the facilitator says: "Now *open* your eyes. Mill and grope. Find a partner and touch-communicate as you did before.

Be aware of your feelings. Is there a difference between your present feelings and those you experienced when you had your eyes closed?

Is the feeling message you are receiving different than before? Try to determine why this is so. Continue groping and milling visually until I tell you to stop."

d. After five minutes, the facilitator stops the exercise and has the group discuss it.

Suggestions for Facilitator Process

Concentrate on the following during processing:

a. How did you feel during the non-visual grope and mill? What feeling messages did you send? How did you send them? What feeling message did you receive? What did your partner do to make you interpret the message as you did?

b. How did you feel during the visual grope and mill? What differences did you perceive in your interactions and reactions between the two types of groping and milling? Most will say they were more self-conscious, more easily distracted, more awkward, etc. during the visual stage. Ask them to delve into the reasons for these feeling differences.

c. Which stage was most enjoyable? Why? Which was most conducive to getting to know other people? Why and how?

Variations
None

WHO?

Subsidiary Goal(s)
a. To explore the process of stereotyping.
b. To give and receive feedback.
c. To examine the significance of visual contact.

Group Application
Twelve members or less. To be used with encounter, personal growth, marathon and t-groups. The exercise is designed to be used during the first hour of the first session. It is particularly effective when used at the first session of an advanced encounter group. Special accommodations and considerations must be made beforehand. (See Administrative Procedure, step *a.*).

Application Variables
One hour. The exercise is 50 per cent non-verbal and 50 per cent verbal. One blindfold is needed for each member.

Administrative Procedure
a. As mentioned above, special accommodations must be made for this exercise. Each member must be blindfolded before entering the room. Since the purpose of the exercise is to expand awareness, ideally no member will have visually seen any other member before entering the room. If it is not pos-

sible to blindfold members at the door, the blindfolds should be put on within the first few minutes of the session.

b. When all members have been blindfolded and led into the room to form a circle, the facilitator makes the following statement: "The reason you have all been blindfolded is to give you an opportunity to get to know some other people in a new way. Hopefully, we will thus avoid the influence of visual stereotypes. Since we don't know one another, I realize it may be difficult to break the ice. Therefore, I would like to suggest that we go around the room and introduce ourselves, using first names only. The blindfold will be left on for one hour. After that time we shall remove them. Please begin by introducing yourselves."

c. After all members have introduced themselves, the facilitator says: "There will be no other structure or directions given to you for the next hour. You may discuss or do anything you feel comfortable with. If you wish to physically touch another member, I suggest that you ask them first. I want to encourage you to try and become aware of your feelings, thoughts and bodily functions."

d. After one hour, the blindfolds are removed and the members discuss the experience.

Suggestions for Facilitator Process

Concentrate on the following during processing:

a. How did you feel at the start of the exercise? What types of impressions did you form on vocal sounds of other members? What did you become aware of when other members spoke?

b. Did you touch anyone? If so, what did you discover about the other member? If not, why not? Do you feel that you got to *know* any other members? If so, who? Why did some members impress you? Did you refuse to allow others to touch you? Why? Why not?

c. What were you aware of during the latter part of the exercise? What type of conversations did the group have? How did you feel when you removed the blindfolds?

Variations

None

*WHOLE BODY EXPLORATION

Subsidiary Goal(s)

a. To learn how one feels about touching and being touched.

b. To develop warmth between members.

Group Application

Twelve members or less. Since dyads are used, group size should be even. To be used only with encounter, personal growth, marathon and t-groups. Best results are obtained when used at the first session of advanced groups. That is, when used with groups whose members have previously experienced the group process and developed some degree of willingness to engaged in touching exercises.[1]

Application Variables

Twenty-five to thirty minutes. The exercise is 100 per cent non-verbal. The room must be large enough to allow the dyads to feel some sense of privacy.

Administrative Procedure

a. The facilitator asks the members to mill around and choose, non-verbally, a partner they would like to get to know better. He tells them to find a spot in the room where they feel comfortable and stand together.

b. When the dyads have been formed, the facilitator says: "Words frequently hinder our getting to know each other. Today we will avoid words and try to know each other using different methods.

Stand as close or as far from your partner as your feelings of warmth for him dictate. Let the distance inform him how close you feel to him.

---

[1]Authors' Note: When used with beginning groups, best results are obtained when used during the second through fourth sessions. When used in this fashion, the primary goal becomes *non-verbal communication*. This, however, does not preclude using the exercise for facilitating the getting acquainted process.

Now, look intently at each other. We all give off warm vibrations. Determine where the warm vibes are coming from. Try to recognize how your partner sends out feelings of warmth."

c. After two or three minutes, he continues: "Now walk toward each other. Close the distance. Fill the space between you with warmth and care.

When you are within touching distance, stop and close your eyes. Determine who will go first. Whoever goes first has three minutes to explore the other person. Do this with your eyes closed. As you explore, try to determine the feelings you have for each other."

d. After three minutes, he says "Switch roles and continue."

e. After three minutes, he says: "Now, engage in mutual exploration. Try to get to know the who of your partner."

f. After three minutes, he says: "Non-verbally, decide who will be the first to receive a back and body massage.

Massage your partner's back and body. As you do this, try to convey your feelings for him. Show him your feelings of trust or distrust, of warmth or coldness, of care or uncaring, and so forth.

As you receive the massage, try to pick up the feelings your partner is conveying through his touch."

g. After five minutes, he says: "Switch positions and continue the massage."

h. After five minutes, he says: "Stand up. Take a minute or two to convey to your partner your feelings for him. Then rejoin the group and we will discuss the experience."

Suggestions for Facilitator Process

Concentrate on the following during processing:

a. What were your criteria for choosing a partner? Ask those who used feeling "hunches" whether these "hunches" proved true. If so, ask why and how.

b. Tell us how your feelings for your partner changed as the exercise progressed. When, why, and how did they change?

c. Which phase did you least enjoy? Why? Which did you most enjoy? Why? Which was most meaningful to you? Why?

d. Tell us about your partner. What vibrations does he emit? How? Describe him as the feeling person you perceive him to be. Do you feel trust and warmth for him? Why? Why not?

Variations

*Variation I

a. To add initial structure, tell the members in step *a* to choose a partner for whom they are experiencing negative or neutral vibrations.

b. Continue as above. During processing investigate the accuracy or inaccuracy of initially perceived vibrations and the reasons for the change in feelings brought about by the exercise.

*WORDS VERSUS HANDS

Subsidiary Goal(s)

a. To learn how one feels about touching and being touched.

b. To learn to tune into tactile exploration and sensations.

c. To develop warmth between members.

Group Application

Group size is unlimited. However, if processing is to occur, the size should be twelve or less. Since dyads are used, group size should be even. Applicable to any group, but most frequently used at the first session of encounter, personal growth, marathon and t-groups.

Application Variables

Fifteen to twenty minutes. The exercise is 70 per cent nonverbal and 30 per cent verbal. The room should be large enough to allow the seated dyads to feel some sense of privacy.

Administrative Procedure

a. The facilitator says: "Non-verbally, find a person you would like to get to know. When you have done this, find a spot in the room and sit down, back-to-back."

b. When this is finished, the facilitator says: "Keep your backs touching. Do not look at each other. Now, take the next five minutes to get to know each other. You are allowed to talk."

c. After five minutes, the facilitator says: "Stop talking. Keep your backs together. Close your eyes and review silently what you learned. After you have done this, decide whether you learned who your partner is or what he is."

d. After two minutes, he says: "Turn and face each other. Touch your knees together. Now, close your eyes, and touch each others hands. Explore your partners hands, palms and fingers. Try to feel the *who* of your partner. Try to let him know the *who* of you. Try not to *think* about him. Just feel the being of him."

e. After five minutes, he says: "Again, sit back to back. Close your eyes and review silently what you learned. After you have done this, decide whether you learned who your partner is or what he is."

f. After two minutes the facilitator has the group discuss the experience.

Suggestions for Facilitator Process

Concentrate on the following during processing:

a. *Concerning the talking stage:* What did you talk about? Usually the talk was intellectual and factual. Ask why emotions and feelings were ignored. Ask if the who or what of the other person was discovered. Inevitably it is the what of him.

b. *Concerning the touching stage:* What feelings did you receive? What did your partner do to send these feelings to you? What feelings were you sending?

c. *Concerning the second back-to-back stage:* What differences between this back-to-back experience and the first. Why? Did you feel you had learned the who or what of your partner? Inevitably it is the who of him. Ask why they learned the *who* with touch and the *what* with words?

d. What feelings did you have toward your partner before we started? What are your feelings now? Why have they changed? What are your reactions to this experience?

Variations

None

V

NON-VERBAL COMMUNICATION

THE PRIMARY GOAL for each exercise in this chapter is to expose members to the various levels at which non-verbal communication can take place. The exercises accomplish this by forcing the participants to *communicate* their thoughts, feelings or reactions at a non-verbal level.

Because they all force the members to engage in non-verbal activities, non-verbal communication is an essential ingredient in almost all of the exercises in this book. The exercises in this chapter, however, are concerned *only* with how and what one communicates to another when words are taboo. One's non-verbal means of communicating are of the utmost importance in these exercises.

As has been pointed out previously, non-verbal means of communicating are *inevitable*. However, they are also subject to misinterpretation. Therefore, the facilitator must rely upon the processing stage to insure that the exercise has created real (instead of errant) learning. A gross injustice occurs whenever you allow a member to leave a session with misperceptions and/or misconceptions. Exhaustive use of processing can eliminate such possibilities.

*AN AWARENESS DIARY

Subsidiary Goal(s)

a. To learn to feel comfortable in non-verbal situations.

b. To learn to pay attention to one's feelings during non-verbal situations.

c. To expose oneself to a variety of stimuli and to learn to report the reactions to such stimuli.

d. To encourage participation.

e. To learn to give and receive feedback.

Group Application

Eight to twelve members. To be used with encounter, personal growth, marathon and t-groups during the middle stages of group development.

Application Variables

One week, fifteen minutes per day per member. The exercise is conducted *outside* the group, usually between sessions. Diary Direction handouts are needed. The facilitator should be aware that processing will take one and a half to two hours.

Administrative Procedure

a. At the end of a session during the middle stage of group development the facilitator hands out Diary Direction handouts.

b. He says: "Read your handouts. You will note that each day for the coming week you are to engage in a specified or unspecified non-verbal activity. This activity is to last *no less* than fifteen minutes. You are to engage in the activity and *immediately* afterwards are to write your feelings, reactions, insights, and any other learnings which strike you as relevant on a piece of eight by five paper. Are there any questions?"

c. The facilitator answers all questions. He then says: "We will see each other next week and read our diaries."

d. At the *start* of the next session the group members share their diaries with the group and discuss the experience.

Suggestions for Facilitator Process

Concentrate on the following during processing:

a. Which day's activity was the easiest for you to engage in? Why? Which was most difficult? Why? Which produced the strangest feelings? Why? Which produced negative or minimal feelings? Which and why?

b. What did you learn about yourself? What was conducive to this learning? How have your feelings about other members changed as a result of hearing their diaries? Why?

c. Who appeared to be the most daring in his non-verbal activities? Why do you say this? Who played it safe? Why do you say this?

Variations

Variation I

a. Instead of using Diary Directions handouts, the facilitator says: "For the next week you are to spend *no less* than fifteen minutes per *day* in engaging in non-verbal activity. Do anything you wish, but avoid "head" or intellectual activities. For example, don't read, do crossword puzzles, watch TV, etc. Try to engage in an activity that awakens your "guts" and senses instead of your brain.

Immediately after completing the activity, write your feelings, reactions, insights, and any other learnings which strike you as relevant on a piece of eight by five paper. The diary reports are to be in the following form":

b. He then gives out handouts of the following example diary entry.

Activity Engaged In	*Feelings, Reactions, Etc.*
I played with shaving cream for fifteen minutes.	I was aware of feeling silly. How could a grown person play with shaving cream? I later began to appreciate the "feel" of the cream. It's smell and aroma really turned me on. Etc.

c. He asks if there are any questions and answers them. He reminds them that they are not to talk during the activities.

DIARY DIRECTIONS[1]

During the next week keep a diary of non-verbal activities. Draw a line down the middle of a piece of eight by five paper. On the left, write the heading "Activity Engaged In" (see example). On the right, write the heading "Feelings, Reactions, Etc." (see example).

---

[1]We urge the facilitator to create non-verbal activities he believes to be more relevant to himself or his group.

Example

Activity Engaged In	*Feelings, Reactions, Etc.*
I played with shaving cream for fifteen minutes.	I was aware of feeling silly. How could a grown person *play* with shaving cream? I later began to appreciate the "feel" of the cream. Its smell and aroma really turned me on. Etc.

You are to engage in the following activities. *Remember,* you are *not* to talk during these activities!

Tomorrow, Day 1: Go to a playground and play. Swing on the swings, slide on the slide, etc.

Day 2: Go where people gather. Remain silent, close your eyes and be aware of what you sense, feel, hear, etc.

Day 3: Go to a wooded area. Close your eyes and be aware of what you sense, feel, hear, etc.

Day 4: Free activity. Do your own non-verbal thing.

Day 5: Find a dog. Play with it. Feel it. Smell it. Hear it. Try to *be* the dog.

Day 6: Look at yourself in a full-length mirror. Spend some time thinking about your body. Then get in tune with what you feel about it. Look at it closely. Be aware of it in its entirety. Be aware of its parts and areas.

Day 7: Free activity. Do your own non-verbal thing.

*BLIND HUGGING[2]

Subsidiary Goal(s)

    a. To facilitate the getting acquainted process.

    b. To increase awareness of one's feelings about touch and body contact.

Group Application

Thirty members or less, although usually applied with groups of twelve or less. To be used with encounter, personal growth,

---

[2]Adapted from an exercise developed by Judy Morris, Counselor, West Intermediate School, Mt. Pleasant, Michigan.

marathon and t-groups. Best results are obtained if used during the early stages of the group's life. However, excellent results can be obtained when applied immediately after a conflict situation or during the closure process.

Application Variables

Fifteen to thirty minutes. The exercise is 100 per cent non-verbal. Blindfolds equal to the size of the group are required. The room must be large enough to allow for comfortable milling. It must also be free of breakable and/or sharp objects which could impede movement.

Administrative Procedure

a. The facilitator asks that all the furniture be moved to the walls.

b. He then says: "I will give each of you a blindfold. Please put it on.

After you have done this, I want you to mill around the room. Hug every person you make contact with. As you hug the person, try to get into contact with him and his being, essence and personality. However, *do not talk* to the person. Use the hug to communicate.

When you are ready to leave that person, part from him and mill around until you make contact with someone else. Hug only one person at a time. Continue milling until you believe you have "sensed" every other member."

Suggestions for Facilitator Process

Concentrate on the following during processing:

a. What were you able to discover about others through their hug? Did you feel anxious or embarrassed? If so, how did you cope with these feelings?

b. Did you only hug, or did you touch faces, hands, torsos, and so on? Why Why not?

c. How did you feel about blindly milling? Did you "look" for someone? Why? What have you learned about yourself and others?

Variations

Variation I

a. Repeat the original exercise. However, at the end of the milling, say: "Continue milling. When you bump into more than one person, hug them all. Maintain the hug until *all* members are hugging en masse."

Variation II

a. Divide the group into two halves. Have one group form an inner circle, facing the other group.

b. Have the outer circle members hug the person in the inner circle who is facing them.

c. Have the outer circle rotate, hug the next inner circle member, rotate again, and so on until all inner circle members have been hugged by all other circle members.

d. Continue reforming circles, hugging and rotating until *all* members have hugged *all* other members.

DISCOUNTING

Subsidiary Goal(s)

a. To emphasize the dynamics involved in minimizing other's feelings.

b. To explore non-verbal messages.

Group Application

Twelve members or less. Since dyads are used, group size should be even. To be used with encounter, personal growth, marathon and t-groups. It is suggested that the exercise be used in the initial stages of the group's life.

Application Variables

Fifteen minutes. The exercise is 50 per cent non-verbal and 50 per cent verbal. The room should be large enough to allow members to spread out unrestrained.

Administrative Procedure

a. The facilitator asks members to mill around and pair off into dyads.

b. The two members are asked to sit down and face one another. The facilitator then gives the following instructions: "I want you to non-verbally cancel out everything you say verbally to your partner. Whatever you say, cancel out its meaning by using gestures, facial expressions, voice fluctuations, laughter, etc. You may discuss anything you wish."

c. After ten minutes the facilitator tells the members to stop, sit quietly and think about the experience.

d. After five minutes the group discusses the experience.

Suggestions for Facilitator Process

Concentrate on the following during processing:

a. How did you and your partner discount your own verbalizations? Was it difficult to do so? Do you recognize any pattern in your behavior which this exemplified? If so what?

b. How did you feel about your partner during this experience? Did you believe what your partner was telling you verbally? How did you cope with the double message being sent to you?

Variations

None

*EAVESDROPPING

Subsidiary Goal(s)

a. To learn to give and receive feedback.

b. To help develop an awareness of body language.

Group Application

Twenty members or less. Applicable to any group, but most frequently used with encounter, personal growth, marathon and t-groups.

Application Variables

Five to seven minutes per dyad observed. The exercise is usually most effective and creates the best learning when three dyads are eavesdropped on. The dyads should be man and man, woman and woman, and man and woman. When conducted in this manner, the group members learn to note if there are differences in non-verbal clues between different types of dyads. The exercise is 20 per cent verbal and 80 per cent non-verbal. Paper and pencils are needed.

Administrative Procedure

a. The facilitator asks for two volunteers. He tells them to go across the room and to engage in a conversation, discussion or argument of no less than three minutes. He tells them: "Try to discuss something which is meaningful to you both. Talk lowly. We are not supposed to be able to hear you. If we can hear you, I'll clap my hands. Lower your voices if you hear my clap."

b. He tells the rest of the group: "We are going to eavesdrop on the dyadic conversation. However, since we won't be able to hear them, we'll have to use other means for guessing what they are discussing. Observe them closely. Look at their non-verbal behavior and body language. Try to guess what they are talking about."

c. The facilitator allows the dyad to converse for no less than three minutes. They should be stopped after five minutes time. The observers are then told: "Write down what you eavesdropped. Write what the dyadic conversation was about."

d. The facilitator has each observer read his guess. The dyad then *briefly* explains what they were talking about.

e. The facilitator can process now or establish another dyad. We recommend establishing another dyad. Vary the composition for each dyad. Repeat the exercise until all three dyads have been eavesdropped upon.

Suggestions for Facilitator Process

Concentrate on the following during processing:

a. *To observers:* What non-verbal behavior and body language cues did you use in making your guesses? Who was correct for dyad one? How do you explain this? Who was wrong about dyad one? Why? Repeat these questions for dyads two and three. Determine whether the dyadic composition had any effect on the observable non-verbal behavior.

b. *To dyads:* How did you choose your topic? How did it feel to be eavesdropped on? What have you learned about your non-verbal and body language behavior?

Variations

None

*EMOTION CARDS

Subsidiary Goal(s)

a. To encourage participation.
b. To learn how non-verbal body cues reflect inner feelings.
c. To learn to observe another's non-verbal behavior.
d. To learn to give and receive feedback.
e. To learn how to tune into one's feelings.

Group Application

Twenty members or less. The group size must be such that subgroups of four or five can be formed. Applicable to any group, but most frequently used with encounter, personal growth, marathon and t-groups.

Application Variables

Twenty to forty minutes. The exercise is 100 per cent non-verbal. A deck of Emotion Cards for each subgroup is needed. See Administrative Procedure step *a* for a description of the Emotion Cards. Emotion Card Game handouts are also needed. The room must be large enough to comfortably accommodate the number of subgroups available.

Administrative Procedure

a. Prior to the use of this exercise, the facilitator develops a sufficient number of Emotion Card sets. An Emotion Card set consists of fifty-two cards. As is the case with regular playing cards, there are four suits and card values from two to ace. The difference is that each card value in the Emotion Card deck represents an emotion. Decks are easily designed by using a felt marker and writing the appropriate emotion on the matching cards of a standard playing deck. The card values and emotions used are as follow.

2	Hope	6	Disgust	10	Dislike
3	Fear	7	Hate	J	Contentment
4	Joy	8	Anger	Q	Despair
5	Depression	9	Passion	K	Temerity
				A	Love

b. When the session starts, the facilitator presents a brief lecturette on non-verbal communication. He should cover at least the following ideas:

   1. Non-verbal communication is more powerful in communicating feelings than are verbal expressions.

   2. It is also ambiguous and difficult to interpret.

   3. To communicate feelings more accurately and effectively, one should develop skill in expressing feelings both verbally and non-verbally.

   4. Frequently one's non-verbal behavior is incongruent with the accompanying verbal expression. Therefore, one goal is to learn to make verbal and non-verbal messages consistent and congruent.

c. He then tells the group they will play a card game designed to facilitate the development of non-verbal communication. He then asks that they non-verbally form subgroups.

d. He distributes the Emotion Card Game handouts, one to each member, and gives each subgroup one deck of Emotion Cards. He asks that they read the handout.

e. After it is clear that all members have read the handouts, the facilitator says: "Are there any questions?" He answers these and then says: "Start playing. Try, as you play, to *feel* the emotions. When your subgroup is finished, return to your original seats and sit quietly until all the subgroups have finished. We will then discuss this experience."

Suggestions for Facilitator Process

Concentrate on the following during processing:

a. Which emotions were hardest to display? Why? Which were easiest? Why? Did any of you express an emotion by touching, hugging, etc. another member? To those who did, why? To those who did not, why?

b. How did you feel at the start of the game? How did your feelings change as the game progressed? When you were expressing a feeling, were you able to experience that feeling? If no, why not? If yes, which feelings and why?

c. Whose feelings were easiest to read? Why? Whose were most difficult to read? Why?

*Variations

Variation I

a. When the facilitator notes that three or more members are having difficulty verbalizing feelings, he has them form a subgroup.

b. He has them sit in a circle within the large group circle. He then has them play a game of Emotion Cards.

c. He tells the observers to watch the player's behavior carefully and to be ready to give them feedback when the game is over.

EMOTION CARD GAME

Object of Game: To Get Rid of All Your Cards.
Method of Play:

1. Deal seven cards to each player.

2. The undealt cards are the draw deck. These are placed face down.

3. The player on the dealer's left selects one of his Emotion cards and lays it face up in front of him.

4. He then non-verbally expresses the emotion represented on the card.

5. Any players whose hands contain the same Emotion card lay them down in front of them.

6. The matched cards are placed in a separate pile, *not* in the draw deck.
7. Any players who did not match the card must draw one from the draw deck. The draw card is placed in the player's hand.
8. If there are no matches, the original player draws a card and the player on his left lays down an Emotion card.
9. Play continues until one player has gotten rid of all of his cards.
10. When the draw deck becomes depleted, the reserve pile (see step 6) is shuffled and it becomes the draw deck.

*EYE MESSAGES

Subsidiary Goal(s)

a. To learn to send and receive feelings, emotions, and messages using only the eyes.
b. To learn to be comfortable in looking another member in the eyes.

Group Application

Twelve members or less. Since dyads are used, group size should be equal. To be used with encounter, personal growth, marathon and t-groups whose members have had sufficient sessions (one to three) to have formed feeling reactions to each other.

Application Variables

Ten to fifteen minutes. The exercise is 100 per cent non-verbal.

Administrative Procedure

a. The facilitator says: "We have been together long enough to have formed impressions of and feelings for each other. Let's learn what it's like to communicate these feelings.

Mill around non-verbally. Look at *every* member. Go to that person you have the most negative and/or neutral feelings for or impressions of and form a dyad."
b. When the dyads are formed, he says: "Sit on the floor facing

your partner. Look into his eyes. Using your eyes, send him messages about your feelings, reactions, and impressions of him. Try to read his messages and react to them by sending answering eye messages. Try to rely *only* on your eyes. Let them do the work. Don't rely on your nose, mouth, etc."

c. After five minutes, the facilitator says: "Mill around and find that person you have the warmest and most positive feelings for and form a dyad."

d. When the dyads are formed, he continues: "Sit on the floor facing your partner. Look into his eyes.

Send and receive eye messages. Let your partner know where he is with you. Find out where you are with him."

e. After five minutes, the facilitator has the group members discuss the experience.

Suggestions for Facilitator Process

Concentrate on the following during processing:

a. *To the first dyads:* What messages did you send? What messages did you think your partner was sending? Why were you inaccurate in reading his message? How do you explain your accuracy? Do you now feel less distant from your partner? If yes, why? If not, why not?

b. *To the second dyads:* How did your messages differ from those you sent your first partner? Why? Do you feel closer to your partner? If yes, why? If not, why not?

c. *To all:* How did you cope with the feelings created by staring into another's eyes. Do you feel more comfortable now in looking into another's eyes? If yes, why? If no, why not?

Variations

*Variation I

a. Have members form dyads.

b. Tell them to spend five minutes verbally exchanging feelings and reactions.

c. After five minutes, tell them to send eye messages to each other. Talking is not allowed.

d. After five minutes, have the group members discuss the experience. Have them compare and contrast the two methods of sending feeling and reaction messages. They will frequently state that the non-verbal eye messages were more moving and meaningful. Have them explore the reasons for this.

*FEELING COMMUNICATION

Subsidiary Goal(s)

a. To learn to give and receive feedback.
b. To learn to be spontaneous in non-verbal communication of feelings.
c. To learn to non-verbally express hidden agendas.

Group Application

Twelve members or less. To be used with encounter, personal growth, marathon and t-groups whose members have had sufficient sessions to have developed warmth, care, and trust for each other.

Application Variables

Time is unlimited and is dictated by the non-verbal expression needs of the members. Most exercises will run approximately thirty minutes. The exercise is 67 per cent non-verbal and 33 per cent verbal.

Administrative Procedure

a. The facilitator says: "Let's take the opportunity to non-verbally relate to each other. We can also use this time to reveal any hidden agendas of a feeling nature which we may be hiding.

Mill around. Move slowly. Take everyone into account. Concentrate on your feelings about yourself, the group, and other members."
b. After a few minutes, he says: "Continue moving. *Whenever* you become aware of a feeling, express it non-verbally.

Don't role play. Don't pretend. Don't *think* about what you should do to express the feeling. Shut off your mind. Let your gut dictate your feeling expression. Be spontaneous."

c. The facilitator should enter the milling group and express his feelings, hugging, dancing, touching, etc. He should, however, be aware of time.

d. The facilitator should stop the group after ten minutes if it appears that the expression of feelings by members is faltering. If the group is still very active after ten minutes, he should allow them to continue until it is clear to him that the step *b* movements are ended.

e. The group members that take ten minutes to discuss the experience. They should talk about how they felt, how they expressed their feelings, how spontaneous they were able to be, and what messages were sent and received.

f. After the ten minutes required in step *e*, the facilitator says: "Let's do it again. This time try to make non-verbal contact with every member."

g. After ten minutes, the facilitator stops the milling and has the group discuss the experience. As has been noted in step *d,* the facilitator should allow the group to continue if he perceives active movement and feeling expression at the ten minute mark.

Suggestions for Facilitator Process

Concentrate on the following during processing:

a. Did your expressions, movements, activities, etc., differ between the two millings? How? Why? In which milling were you most spontaneous? Why?

b. What types of feelings did you experience? How did you express these? Did you fail to express any? Which feelings and why?

c. What have you learned about yourself? What have you learned about other members? Was the experience of value to you? If yes, how and why? If no, why not?

Variations

None

*GIVING-RECEIVING OF TACTILE COMMUNICATION[3]

Subsidiary Goal(s)

  a. To recognize the potentiality of pleasure to be found in giving and receiving tactile stimulation.
  b. To determine the extent that touch creates anxiety or embarrassment in oneself.

Group Application

Twelve members or less. Since dyads are used, group size should be even. To be used with encounter, personal growth, marathon and t-groups. Most effective when used after the members have developed feelings of warmth and care for each other. An equal number of males to females makes for the most effective utilization of the exercise and its variations.

Application Variables

Ten minutes. The exercise is 100 per cent non-verbal. The room must be large enough to allow the dyads some feeling of privacy.

Administrative Procedure

  a. The facilitator asks that the group mill, non-verbally, and form dyads. He may wish to add: "Form a dyad with someone you feel close to and for whom you have warm, positive feelings."
  b. The facilitator says: "One of you is to sit on the floor. The other is to kneel behind you. Both are to keep their eyes closed throughout the entire experience. Please remove obstructive outer clothing such as your coats, sweaters over blouses, and so forth."
  c. He tells the kneelers: "You are to show your partner how much you care for him by rubbing his neck, shoulders, upper and lower back."

---

[3]Adapted from an exercise developed by Dan Millar, Coordinator of Interpersonal and Public Communication, Central Michigan University.

d. He says to the seated members: "Concentrate on the sensations your skin is receiving. Be aware of your feelings and reactions. Try to determine what messages your partner is sending to you."

e. After five minutes, roles are reversed and step *c* is repeated.

Suggestions for Facilitator Process

Concentrate on the following during processing:

a. *To seated members:* Did you feel your partner cared for you? Why do you feel this way? If you could have directed his tactile movements, what would you have told him to do? Why? Did you feel embarrassed, anxious, or sexually stimulated? How did you cope with these feelings?

b. *To kneelers:* What were your feelings as you touched your partner? What were your feelings for him? How did you try to convey them to him?

c. *To all:* Have your feelings for your partner changed? How? Why? What did you learn about yourself and your partner?

Variations

*Variation I

a. Divide the group into triads so that the giving and receiving can be simultaneous.

b. During processing, ask whether there was frustration over not being able to "give" to the person "giving to you," whether it was difficult to give and receive at the same time, and if the messages sent and received changed in intesity during the five minutes.

*Variation II

a. Divide the group into same sex dyads, men with men and females with females,

b. Repeat the original exercise procedure.

c. During processing, investigate how being with a same sex partner affected the intensity and style of tactile communication.

*Variation III

a. Divide the group into dyads based on distance, neutrality or

negativeness of partner feelings.
b. Repeat the original exercise procedure.
c. During processing, concentrate on changes in feelings for each other and the reasons for such changes.
*Variation IV
a. Divide the group into male-female dyads.
b. Repeat the original exercise procedure.
c. During processing, concentrate on whether sexual feelings were present, why they occurred and how the members coped with them.

*HEAD CARE

Subsidiary Goal(s)

a. To learn how effective touch can be in communicating feelings.
b. To give and receive feedback.
c. To help develop sensory awareness.

Group Application

Twelve members or less. Since dyads are used, group size should be even. To be used with encounter, personal growth, marathon and t-groups whose members have developed a warm and caring atmosphere.

Application Variables

Ten minutes. The exercise is 100 per cent non-verbal. The room must be large enough to allow the dyads to spread out without feeling unduly restricted.

Administrative Procedure

a. The facilitator says: "Form dyads. Try to pick a partner whom you feel close to."
b. When the dyads are formed, he continues: "One of you is to sit on the floor. The other is to lay down, on his back, and place his head in the lap of the seated partner."
c. The facilitator then says: "The seated partner is going to "care" for the head in his lap. Try to be aware of your own

feelings and reactions as you "care for" or are "cared for." Try to communicate to your partner your feelings for him."

d. After five minutes, roles are reversed and step *c* is repeated.

Suggestions for Facilitator Process

Concentrate on the following during processing:

a. How do you feel about this experience? What have you learned about yourself and your partner? How and why have your feelings for each other changed? Which was most enjoyable and meaningful, caring or being cared for?

b. *To senders:* What feeling messages were you sending? How did you feel during the experience?

c. *To receivers:* What messages were you receiving? What was happening in your body?

Variations

*Variation I

a. Form the dyads based on feelings of distance, negativism or neutrality.

b. Repeat the original exercise procedure.

c. During processing, concentrate on the direction of changes in partners' feelings and the reasons for such changes.

*Variation II

a. Form same sex dyads, men with men and women with women.

b. Repeat the original exercise procedure.

c. During processing, concentrate on how being with a same sex partner affected the intensity of the non-verbal, tactile communication and why it affected the procedure.

*HUGGING—WARM AND COLD

Subsidiary Goal(s)

a. To develop warmth between participants.

b. To learn how one feels about touching and being touched.

Group Application

Twelve members or less. Since dyads are used, group size should be equal. Although applicable to any group, effective results are seldom obtained with groups other than encounter, personal growth, marathon and t-groups whose members have had sufficient sessions (one to three) to have formed feeling reactions to each other.

Application Variables

Five to ten minutes. The exercise is 100 per cent non-verbal.

Administrative Procedure

a. The facilitator tells the members: "We have been together long enough to have formed impressions of and feelings for each other. Let's learn what it's like to communicate these feelings.

   Mill around non-verbally. Look at *every* member. Go to that person you have the most negative and/or neutral feelings for or impressions of and form a dyad."

b. When the dyads are formed, he says: "Hug each other. Show your feelings for each other. Don't *fake* it."

c. When it becomes apparent that step *b* is completed, he says: "Mill around and find that member you have the warmest or most positive feelings for and form a dyad."

d. When the dyads are formed, he says: "Hug each other. Show your feelings for each other. Don't *fake* it."

e. When step *d* is completed, the facilitator says: "Go back to your original partners."

f. When the dyads are formed, he continues: "Hug each other. Show your feelings for each other. Don't *fake* it."

g. When this is completed, he has the group discuss the experience.

Suggestions for Facilitator Process

Concentrate on the following during processing:

a. How did you decide your first partner choice? What was that hug like? For example, was it warm, cold, mechanical, etc?

b. How did you decide your second partner choice? How and why was that hug different? For example, was it longer, warmer, more mechanical, etc., and why?

c. Was the second hug with your first partner different? How and why? If not, why not? What have you learned about hugging as a means of communicating feelings?

Variations

*Variation I

a. Ask for a volunteer. Have him stand in the center of the group circle.
b. Then say: "We all have positive or negative feelings, reactions, and impressions for this member. All of you who have negative or neutral feelings for him come forward and give him a group hug. Be honest. Don't fail to participate if you have negative or neutral reactions or feelings."
c. When the group hug is ended, the facilitator says: "Those of you who have positive feelings for this member come forward and give him a group hug."
d. After the group hug, processing occurs. It should concentrate on the volunteer's reactions to and perceptions of the two hugs. Attention should also be given to members who failed to participate. Why did they do so?
e. All other members who wish this experience should be given the opportunity to do so.

*Variation II

a. Whenever a member is perceived as being too negative in his self-concept and self-evaluation, the facilitator asks him to enter the center of the circle.
b. He then has the group give the member a group hug, saying: "Show this person how dear he is to you. Show him how much you care for him."
c. Such an action will help the member to begin to develop feelings of self-worth.

*Variation III

a. Whenever a member is perceived as being too positive in his self-concept and self-evaluation, the facilitator asks him to enter the center of the circle.
b. He then tells the group to give the member a group hug, saying: "We all don't feel (name the member) is as great as

he appears to believe himself to be. Show him your feelings in your hug."

c. Such a hug will usually be cool, restricted, and non-committal. This will help the member learn that he *does not* come on warm and positive to all the members. Such learning can help him develop a more honest system of self-evaluation.

*NON-VERBAL CHARADES

Subsidiary Goal(s)

a. To help develop an awareness of body language.
b. To develop a feeling of accomplishment.
c. To encourage participation.
d. To learn to give and receive feedback.

Group Application

Twenty members or less. The group size must be such that subgroups of four or five can be formed. Applicable to any group. Especially effective when used with classrooms and t-groups whenever learning about body language and non-verbal communication are matters of concern.

Application Variables

Twenty to thirty minutes. The exercise is 90 per cent non-verbal and 10 per cent verbal. Situation Cards sufficient for the number of subgroups are needed. See Administrative Procedure, step *a* for an explanation and examples of Situation Cards. Paper and pencils are also needed.

Administrative Procedure

a. Before the session starts, the facilitator prepares Situation Cards. Situation Cards are three by five cards on which charade situations are typed.
   Examples of some Situation Cards are:
   1. You have just had a minor auto accident. You think the other driver is at fault. He thinks you are at fault. The other members may be passengers or eye-witnesses.

2. Your subgroup is playing bridge. One of you believes the other committed a tragic mistake while playing his cards. He feels his play was justified. Do not include the action of the game in your charade!

3. Your subgroup is a board of trustees. You are to decide who will be president, who treasurer, who secretary, etc.

The facilitator should feel free to invent any situations he feels are relevant to his group. Be sure, however, to invent situations which will require non-verbal communication and not action. If action would give away the situation (see example two), place a warning on the Situation Card similar to that found in example two.

b. When the group convenes, the facilitator says: "Non-verbally form subgroups of (name the number)."

c. When this is completed, he says: "We are going to engage in a non-verbal charades exercise. The purpose is to help us improve our awareness of non-verbal communication.

I am going to give each subgroup one Situation Card. You will have five minutes to practice your presentation. You may practice here or in another room. Remember, the practice and presentation are to be non-verbal."

d. When the subgroups are ready, the facilitator says: "Make your presentations."

e. After each subgroup's presentation, the facilitator tells the observing members to write down on their paper what they believe the presented situation to be.

f. After each presentation, the observers read their situation guesses. The facilitator then reads the subgroup's Situation Card.

g. When all the presentations have been completed, the facilitator has the group discuss the experience.

Suggestions for Facilitator Process

Concentrate on the following during processing:

a. First have the observers discuss their guesses. Discuss the reasoning behind the guesses. Ask what non-verbal behavior and body language cues were used to help make guesses. Investigate the dynamics involved in correct and incorrect guessing.

b. *To subgroups:* What behavior did you observe in your subgroup's practice session? What feelings do you believe were present? What non-verbal behavior did you use to support your belief. How did you feel when you discovered most of us guessed your situation correctly? How did you feel when you discovered most of us guessed incorrectly?

c. *To all:* What have you learned about non-verbal communication and body language? Which presentation did you enjoy the most? Why? Which was most difficult to guess? why?

Variations

*Variation I

a. Form subgroups. Then explain the exercise as above and read some *possible* situations to the group.

b. Have a subgroup develop and practice in front of the group a situation of their own making. Tell them not to use your examples, but rather to create one of their own. This development is to be non-verbal.

c. After their development and practice, have the entire group discuss the experience. Concentrate on roles observed in the subgroup, non-verbal behavior exhibited, and the means of communicating to each other what situation to portray.

d. Continue the exercise until all subgroups have experienced the development and practice phase. Process after *each* presentation.

*NON-VERBAL WORD CREATIONS

Subsidiary Goal(s)

a. To develop an awareness of group unity.

b. To learn to give and receive feedback.

c. To learn about member roles.

d. To encourage participation.

Group Application

Twenty members or less. The exercise utilizes subgroups of four or five, so the group size must be such that four and/or five person subgroups may be formed. Applicable to any group.

Application Variables

Twenty to thirty minutes per word creation. Each subgroup will use approximately two minutes. The exercise is 100 per cent non-verbal. A blackboard is needed.

Administrative Procedure

a. The facilitator asks that the members non-verbally form subgroups of (name the number). As they do this he writes the following words on the blackboard:

Garbage	Sex	Day
Life	Time	Strength
Dependency	Lust	Love

b. When the subgroups are formed, the facilitator says: "Each of the subgroups will have to present, non-verbally, a drama, play, or other creation for the word (insert word chosen). You are to do this as a team. You have five minutes to practice. You can practice here or in another room. However, practice *non-verbally* and be back here in five minutes!"
c. When the subgroups practice time is over, the facilitator says: "Make your presentations."
d. After all presentations have been made, the facilitator can process the exercise or give the group another word to create.

Suggestions for Facilitator Process

Concentrate on the following during processing:
a. Which presentation did you enjoy the most? Why? Which did you least enjoy? Why?
b. What roles were evident in your subgroup as it used its five minute practice time? Did you feel competitive? If yes, why? If no, why not?
c. What feelings did you experience during the practice ses-

sion? During the presentations? Why did your presentation ignore touching? How did you feel about those presentations which used touch?

Variations

*Variation I

a. The facilitator repeats step *a* of the original exercise.
b. He then says: "Each of the subgroups will have to present, non-verbally, a drama, play, or other creation for one of the words on the board. We will use whichever word you decide upon. You have five minutes to reach consensus and inform me of which word we will use. Remember, this consensus is to be done non-verbally."
c. When the time is up, the facilitator determines the word decided upon, and continues the original exercise, starting at step *b*.
d. During processing, concentrate on the method of reaching consensus, the significance of the word chosen, and the reasons for choosing the word. For example, why was love chosen instead of sex, lust, etc.?

*PANTOMIME

Subsidiary Goal(s)

a. To gain greater awareness of non-verbal cues.
b. To provide an opportunity to explore creativity.
c. To give and receive feedback.

Group Application

Twelve members or less. To be used with encounter, personal growth, marathon and t-groups. Best results are obtained if the exercise is used in the advanced stage of the group's life.

Application Variables

Forty-five minutes to one hour. The exercise is 100 per cent non-verbal. The room must be large enough to allow subgroups to work in semi-privacy.

Administrative Procedure

a. The facilitator asks members to non-verbally pair off into two subgroups of six members or less.

b. The two subgroups are asked to find separate spots within the same room and are then given the following instrutcions: "I would like each member in the subgroup to present a pantomime about himself and his relationships with the other members in the subgroup. Only one member is to perform at a time."

c. Instructions should not exceed the specifics given above, for it is suggested that the less specific structure given the greater the amount of creativity.

d. Each member is allowed up to ten minutes to perform his pantomime.

e. After both subgroups have finished, the experience is processed.

Suggestions for Facilitator Process

Concentrate on the following during processing:

a. How did you deal with the ambiguity of the instructions? How did you decide what to present to your subgroup? Do you feel you were effective in your presentation? If yes, why? If no, why not?

b. Did you have much physical contact within your subgroups? Why? Why not? What have you discovered about the other members in your subgroup? About yourself?

Variations

*Variation I

a. Ask for a volunteer.

b. Give him the instructions stated in step *b* of the original exercise.

c. After he has finished, process his exercise.

d. Continue until all who wish the experience have had the opportunity to do so.

*SHOW AND TELL

Subsidiary Goal(s)

a. To gain greater awareness of members' resources.
b. To produce an environment conducive to creativity.
c. To increase non-verbal awareness.

Group Application

Twelve members or less. To be used with any group concerned with the exploration of creativity and sharing.

Application Variables

One hour. The exercise is 100 per cent non-verbal. The room must be large enough to accommodate two to three subgroups in semi-privacy.

Administrative Procedure

a. The facilitator asks members to non-verbally divide into subgroups of four to six members.
b. The subgroups are given the following instructions: "I want you to create a presentation for the other members in the group. I will give you a word and you are to *non-verbally* create a representation of that word by using all members in your subgroup. After fifteen minutes, we will come back and form a large group and will view the presentations. Again, all presentations are to be presented and performed non-verbally."
c. The facilitator gives the same word to the subgroups (e.g. life, time, garbage, meaningful, love, if, etc.).
d. After fifteen minutes, the subgroup presents to the rest of the group.
e. If time allows, after all presentations are given, another word may be given to the subgroups for presentation.
f. The members then discuss the experience.

Suggestions for Facilitator Process

Concentrate on the following during processing:

a. Who took the leadership roles in your subgroup? Were you

satisfied with the creation your subgroup came up with? Do you feel you got your message across to the large group? If not, why not? How did you contribute to the presentation?

b. What impressions and perceptions did you have of the other subgroups? What have you learned from or about the other members in the group? Did you have fun? Were you surprised at the creative resources which are within each one of us?

Variations

Variation I

a. Instead of giving the subgroups a specific word, the facilitator asks members to simply create.
b. The same basic procedure as described in the original exercise is then followed.

Variation II

a. The facilitator gives a different word to each subgroup.
b. After presentations, the facilitator asks that the observing members guess what the "word" was.

*SILENCE IS GOLDEN

Subsidiary Goal(s)

a. To gain greater insight into the dynamics involved in feedback.
b. To further enhance awareness of non-verbal cues.
c. To explore the different meanings of silence.

Group Application

Twelve members or less. To be used with encounter, personal growth, marathon and t-groups. Best results are obtained if the exercise is used in the advanced stage of a group's life.

Application Variables

Two hours. The exercise is 100 per cent non-verbal.

Administrative Procedure

a. The facilitator may wish to give a brief lecturette on the value and importance of non-verbal communication.

   b. He then tells the members that for the next two hours there will be *no* verbal communication.
   c. Members are asked to participate as normal, without talking, (i.e. expression of feelings, thoughts, feedback, and ideas).
   d. After the two hours the members discuss the experience.

Suggestions for Facilitator Process

Concentrate on the following during processing:

   a. What types of feelings did you have when I told you there would be no talking? What did you gain from this experience? How soon did these feelings pass, if they passed at all?
   b. What have you learned about the other members in the group? What have you learned about yourself? Was it difficult for you to express your feelings? Why? To give and receive feedback? Why?
   c. What meanings does silence have for you now? Do you feel you are more aware of non-verbal cues? If yes, how? If no, why not?

Variations

Variation I

   a. Vary the amount of time allowed for the silence. However, it is suggested that a minimum of one hour be allowed.

*THE SELF AND OTHERS

Subsidiary Goal(s)

   a. To investigate the dynamics involved in giving and receiving.
   b. To learn to observe non-verbal behavior.
   c. To give and receive feedback.

Group Application

Twelve or less. The exercise utilizes a quintet. All the other group members are observers. Applicable to any group, but most frequently used with encounter, personal growth, marathon and t-groups.

Application Variables

Twenty to twenty-five minutes. The exercise is 100 per cent non-verbal. A large covered box is needed. The box is to be filled with a variety of common and uncommon objects. We recommend an assortment similar to the following:

a newspaper	a quarter	a frisby
a plastic spoon	a one dollar bill	a roll of toilet
a penny	a can opener	paper
a nickel	some rocks	a Playboy
a dime	a cigar	centerfold
an onion	an unused diary	

Administrative Procedure

a. When the facilitator notes that one or more of the members are having difficulty communicating with the group, he says: "You (name the member or members) are having some difficulty communicating with us. Most of us have little idea of where we are with you. So that we may find this out and you may improve your communication, I want you to choose any other members you wish, for whatever reason you wish, and form a five person subgroup. Do this non-verbally."

b. When the subgroup is formed, the facilitator has them sit in the middle of the large group circle. He gives the box to *whichever* member he perceives as having the greatest communication difficulty.

c. He then tells the member: "This box and its contents are yours. You can do with it and the contents whatever you wish. You may keep all the objects, or you may give some or all of them away. If, however, you give objects away, have a reason for doing so."

d. The facilitator tells the observing group to watch the subgroup members carefully and to be ready to give them feedback on their non-verbal behavior when the exercise has been completed.

e. After twenty or twenty-five minutes, the subgroup will have finished its activity. The facilitator stops the exercise and has the group discuss the experience.

Suggestions for Facilitator Process

Concentrate on the following during processing:

a. *To the member who controlled the box:* What feelings did you experience during the exercise? Why did you give (name the member) the item you did? You will find that much can be learned when you explore the reasons for giving. Feel free to ask this last question for each item.

b. *To the other subgroup members:* What feelings did you experience? How did you (name the member) feel when you were given the (name the item)? Again, repeat this question for all of the items, for much can be learned about the members and their group relationships.

c. *To the observers:* What feedback can you give the subgroup members? Have your feelings for them changed as a result of today? If so, how and why?

*Variations

Variation I

a. When the facilitator notes that a member is unwilling to self-disclose and/or has communication problems, he gives the member the box and repeats the directions found in step *c* of the original exercise.

VI

REJECTION

THE PRIMARY GOAL for each exercise in this chapter is to expose the group and its members to the dynamics involved in rejecting and being rejected.

Rejection exercises are quite stressful. However, they are frequently used to help members deal with the concept of rejection. The appropriateness of the use of such exercises is totally contingent upon the facilitator's discretion. He should have reason for exposing the group and its members to a rejection experience.

The rejection concept is a difficult dynamic to deal with for group members. Because of this, many facilitators overlook the use of the rejection experience. Yet, rejection in life is a reality and members should learn how to cope with it.

We believe rejection exercises can often lead to increased self-awareness, deeper interpersonal relationships, and greater insight into the coping behavior of oneself and of fellow members.

Because of the stress placed on individuals involved in a rejection exercise, the facilitator is asked to pay particular attention to the processing stage.

*COME JOIN US

Subsidiary Goal(s)

a. To learn how one copes with anxiety and acceptance.

Group Application

Twelve members or less. To be used only with encounter, personal growth, marathon and t-groups. Most effective when used during the middle or latter stages of the group's life.

Application Variables

Five to ten minutes. The exercise is 100 per cent non-verbal.

119

Administrative Procedure

a. The facilitator, prior to the session, informs *one* member of the exercise.

b. At the start of the session, the facilitator says: "(Name the member) has brought me an interesting problem solving exercise. He and I will need some of you to help us solve it. We will discuss between us who we want. We'll be picking those of you who we feel are creative, intelligent and insightful."

c. The facilitator and the member then discuss between them which members they will choose. They are to do this quietly enough that the members *cannot* hear their words. They should point at members, shake their heads, shrug their shoulders and engage in other non-verbal cues which indicate acceptance and rejection.

They indicate whom they are choosing and ask the member to sit somewhere else. This continues until they have a group of "chosen" members and a group of "unchosen." (In a group of twelve, you would usually leave three or four in the unchosen group) .

They then join the "chosen" group and quietly inform them about what has been happening. After a few minutes they reform the group and tell the "unchosen" what has occurred.

Suggestions for Facilitator Process

Concentrate on the following during processing:

a. *To the chosen:* How did you feel before you were chosen? How did you cope with these feelings? How did you feel after we chose you? *To the first chosen:* How did you feel about being chosen first? *To the last chosen:* How did you feel about being chosen last?

b. *To the unchosen:* How did you feel as you saw others being picked? How did you feel about being unchosen? What have you learned about how you cope with rejection?

c. *To all:* What have you learned about yourself as a result of this experience? What feelings did you have toward (name the member) and me? Investigate the reasons for differences in feelings toward him as opposed to those held for you.

Variations
None

*INCLUDE YOURSELF

Subsidiary Goal(s)
a. To develop group unity.
b. To develop feelings of warmth and acceptance among the members.
c. To learn that inclusion requires individual effort and commitment.

Group Application
Twelve members or less. To be used only with encounter, personal growth, marathon and t-groups whose members have developed rapport between and insight into each other.

Application Variables
Two to five minutes. The exercise is 100 per cent non-verbal.

Administrative Procedure
a. Whenever the facilitator notices that a member is unwilling to become part of the group, appears to feel that others should "let him in" without effort on his part, is getting considerable feedback from others as to his "exclusion" attitude, or feels rejected by the group, the facilitator asks him to stand outside the group circle.
b. He tells the member: "You appear to believe it's our job to get you in the group. That's a lot of shit. If you want in, earn it. You will have to break into the center of our circle. We want you in, but we want you to *earn* it, to *try* for it."
c. He tells the members: "Those of you who feel that (name the member) should earn and put forth his *own* effort to be part of us, form a circle. Hold each others waists tightly.

Make the circle a strong chain which he cannot break. Do your best to keep him out of the circle."

d. The facilitator joins the group circle. He then tells the member: "If you feel rejected by us, fight it. Don't grovel, beg, or expect us to let you in. Earn the right to membership! Break into the circle and *include yourself*. We, who want you to be part of us, but are unwilling to *hand* that membership to you, will do our best to keep you out."

e. After the member has broken in, the facilitator and the others give the member a group hug. If the member tries but is unable to break in, the facilitator steps back and says: "Join us. You tried. That is all we asked. Simply try." He and the group then give the member a group hug.

Suggestions for Facilitator Process

Concentrate on the following during processing:

a. *To the member:* How did you feel as you tried to break in? Why do you think we resisted your efforts so vigorously? *Point out:* if we wanted you to get your way and not *earn* your way, we would have allowed you an easy entrance. How do you feel now about you as a part of us?

b. *To the others:* How did you feel during the inclusion attempt? Did you *let* him in? If yes, why? If not, why not? Usually, the members resisted because they wanted the member to get the message "we want you with us, but you must *try*, you must *earn* it." How do you feel now about the member?

c. Ask any members who did not participate why they chose to watch instead of involving themselves.

Variations

None

*REJECTION

Subsidiary Goal(s)

a. To learn to cope with the feelings created when one rejects another person.

b. To learn to cope with risk taking behavior.

c. To learn to non-verbally "unload" hidden agendas.

d. To learn to recognize how feelings of acceptance differ from feelings of rejection.

Group Application

Twelve members or less. To be used with encounter, personal growth, marathon and t-groups whose members have had sufficient sessions to have developed feeling reactions to each other.

Application Variables

Ten to fifteen minutes. The exercise is 100 per cent non-verbal.

Administrative Procedure

a. The facilitator says: "We have been together long enough to have developed some positive and negative feelings for and reactions to each other.

Let's take the the opportunity to learn to non-verbally express these feelings. Mill around and look at your fellow members. As you do this, be aware of the positive and negative feelings and reactions you have toward them."

b. After a minute, the facilitator continues: "Now, spread out. Go to each other. Using non-verbal means of communication, invite the other person to accept you.

When a member approaches seeking acceptance, look into yourself and gauge your feelings for him. If you have *any* negative feelings or reactions for the person, non-verbally *reject* him. Try to show him through your rejection the extent of your negative feelings.

If, after having gauged your feelings, you can *honestly* say you have *no* negative feelings or reactions to him, hug him.

Continue inviting, rejecting, and accepting until you have made contact with all the members."

c. After it becomes apparent that the step *b* movements are completed, the facilitator has the group discuss the experience.

Suggestions for Facilitator Process

Concentrate on the following during processing:

a. How did you invite acceptance? Did you change your method for inviting acceptance as the exercise progressed? How and why? How did it feel to be accepted?

b. How did you reject others? How did it feel to reject others? Did you accept anyone you should, according to the exercise guidelines, have rejected? Why?

c. Who was rejected the most? Why? Who was accepted the most? Why?

Variations

None

*RIGGED REJECTIONS

Subsidiary Goal(s)

a. To learn to cope with risk taking behavior.

b. To learn to cope with the feelings created when one rejects another person.

Group Application

Twelve members or less. To be used only with encounter, personal growth, marathon and t-groups whose members have had sufficient sessions to have developed feelings of warmth, care, and acceptance for each other. The exercise is particularly effective when used in a t-group whenever the facilitator wants the members to learn about rejection.

Application Variables

Five to ten minutes. The exercise is 100 per cent non-verbal. A maze drawing and a pencil are needed. Maze drawings are readily available in puzzle and game books. The maze drawing should be reproduced on a large piece of paper or cardboard so that observers can easily see it.

Administrative Procedure

a. Prior to the start of the group, the facilitator tells three members: "We will be engaging in a rejection exercise today. I want you to help me.

I will ask for volunteers to solve a maze puzzle. Put up your hands and I'll pick you. I will tell you three to work non-verbally as a team and solve the maze. When you are engaged in this task, fail! Do as much wrong as you can. Be *obviously* wrong.

The others will be told to observe your actions and urged to non-verbally offer you help and assistance. Non-verbally reject and scorn *every* offer.

b. When the group starts, the facilitator says: "Let's do an exercise in observation of teamwork. I have a maze and a pencil. Can I have three volunteers who will work as a team in non-verbally solving the maze?"

c. He chooses the "rigged" members and tells them: "Your task will be to work non-verbally as a team and solve this maze."

d. He then tells the other members: "Circle around the triad so you can see what they are doing. Observe their non-verbal interaction."

e. He tells the triad to begin. After two minutes, he says: "It appears the triad is having problems. Somebody help them. But, make sure your help is of a non-verbal nature."

f. Members will begin to offer aid and be rejected. When it becomes evident that the observers have ceased to offer aid, the facilitator stops the exercise, explains it was rigged, and has the group discuss the experience.

Suggestions for Facilitator Process

Concentrate on the following during processing:

a. *To the observers:* How did you feel when your assistance was rejected and scorned? How did you cope with these feelings? Why did some of you fail to offer aid? (They will usually respond that they did not want to be rejected.) *Ask:* do you usually fail to take a chance because of fear of rejection? Why?

b. *To the triad:* How did you feel about rejecting others? How did you cope with these feelings? Which members were difficult to reject? Why? Which members were easily rejected? Why do you say this?

c. *To all:* What have you learned about you and rejection? What have you learned about your willingness to take a chance?

Variations

None

*WANDERING ALONE

Subsidiary Goal(s)

a. To learn that acceptance is *earned* through one's effort and is not *given* to one.

b. To learn to take the risk of asking for inclusion.

Group Application

Twelve members or less. To be used only with encounter, personal growth, marathon and t-groups whose members have had sufficient sessions to have developed feelings of warmth, care, and trust for each other.

Application Variables

Three to five minutes per "wanderer" (see Administrative Procedure, step *b*). The exercise is 100 per cent non-verbal.

Administrative Procedure

a. Whenever the facilitator notices that a member feels uncertain as to his acceptance in the group, the facilitator says: "I get a feeling that you are not sure whether we accept or reject you. Let's see if a non-verbal exercise can help you discover an answer to your question."

b. He tells the members, excluding the member in question, to form a circle with their arms around each other's waists. He tells the member: "We are together. You are outside of us. You are a 'wanderer'."

Wander around the room. Explore it. Concentrate on your feelings as you wander. Do you feel free and unencumbered? Do you feel rejected? Do you feel alone? Concentrate on feelings such as these.

When you are ready to join us, come to us. We *will* accept you because we care for you and want you with us. Wander until you feel you *want* to be part of us."

c. The facilitator joins the circle. When the "wanderer" joins it, the facilitator and the group give him a group hug. They all then discuss the experience.

Suggestions for Facilitator Process

Concentrate on the following during processing:

a. *To the "wanderer"*: How did you feel as you wandered? Have him explore the reasons for his feelings. Do you now feel more a part of us? If so, why? If not, why not? Do you feel more accepted by us? If so, why? If not, why not?

b. *To the others*: How did you feel as he wandered? Did you want to go to him and bring him to us? If yes, why? If no, why not? Do you now feel more warmth and acceptance for the member? If yes, why? If not, why not?

Variations

None

VII

RELAXATION AND PLAY

THE PRIMARY GOAL for each exercise in this chapter is to provide a structure which allows for both relaxation and play (or fun).

We believe that 'hard' play is an extremely important yet often overlooked dynamic within the group structure. Playing can help create creative and constructive paths for 'letting go' of self-control. The following exercises were not designed to provide easy access for avoidance behavior but rather to shed new light on often long lost experiences. It has been our experience that play and relaxation can *often* bring about levels of understanding and insight into both self and others which are unique.

The facilitator should give careful consideration to the appropriateness of the following exercises. It is our suggestion that implementation take place after long involved encounters in which members have become emotionally drained. We have found that processing of relaxation and play exercises is not always appropriate or necessary. This however is up to the facilitator's discreation.

*CARPET ROLL

Subsidiary Goal(s)

a. To learn to "let go" and have fun.

Group Application

Twenty members or less. Applicable to any group. The exercise is quite effective when used near the end of an emotionally charged or highly confrontive session of encounter, personal growth, marathon or t-groups.

Application Variables

Ten to fifteen minutes. The exercise is 100 per cent non-verbal. A carpeted room is needed.

Administrative Procedure

a. Near the end of a session in which members were highly confrontive, emotionally involved, etc., the facilitator says: "Let's do something silly to help us get rid of some of our tensions."

b. He continues: "Lie on the floor. Separate sufficiently so you won't roll into each other."

c. When all members are in position, he says: "Put your arms by your sides. Now roll around on the carpeting. Roll fast. Then roll slowly. Let your tensions drain off."

d. After a minute or two, he says: "Now, lie on the floor side by side. Place your head next to the other person's feet. Pack tightly. Become a human carpet." (See photograph sequence on pages 132-133.)

e. When this is completed, the facilitator says: "You, (name the member on one end of the line), get up and roll on the human carpet. Roll from your end to the other.
When you get to the other end, lie down and take the end position. Then you, (name the person now at the vacated end), roll on the human carpet.
Continue until all have rolled on the human carpet."

f. When everyone completes step *e,* the group can disperse or process the experience.

Suggestions for Facilitator Process

Concentrate on the following during processing:

a. *Regarding the real carpet roll:* Did it help relax you? Why? Why not? How did you feel as you did it?

b. *Regarding the human carpet roll:* How did it differ from your first roll? Was it more or less relaxing? Why?

Variations

None

*CHINESE PUZZLE

Subsidiary Goal(s)

a. To explore the dynamics involved in play.

b. To explore members' feelings about close physical contact.

Group Application

Any number of members. To be used with any group. Best results are obtained if the exercise is used after intense interaction has occurred.

Application Variables

Ten minutes. The exercise is 60 per cent non-verbal and 40 per cent verbal. The room must be large enough to allow members to move about unrestrained.

Administrative Procedure

a. The facilitator asks the group for a volunteer who is willing to solve a puzzle. The volunteer is then asked to leave the room.

b. The facilitator now asks the rest of the members to stand up, form a circle, and join hands.

c. The group is told to interwind themselves as completely as possible without breaking contact (e.g. going under, around, above each other, etc.).

d. The group should now appear to be a mass of closely knit bodies. (See photograph sequence on pages 134-136.).

e. The volunteer is brought back into the room and is to verbally, *not* physically, instruct members to untangle without breaking contact at any time.

f. After the circle is reformed the group members discuss the experience.

Suggestions for Facilitator Process

Concentrate on the following during processing:

a. *To the members:* How did you feel about the close physical contact between yourself and others? Did you want to become untangled? How did you contribute to making the "puzzle" complex?

b. *To the volunteer:* What type of strategy did you use? Did you feel left out? What was your first impression as you entered the room?

Variations

None

Figure 7-2. Carpet Roll

Figure 7-3. Carpet Roll

Figure 7-4. Carpet Roll

Figure 7-5. Carpet Roll

Figure 7-6. Chinese Puzzle

Figure 7-7. Chinese Puzzle.

Figure 7-8. Chinese Puzzle

Figure 7-9. Chinese Puzzle

Figure 7-10. Chinese Puzzle

*CIRCLE AND STAR

Subsidiary Goal(s)

a. To allow members the opportunity to encounter the fantasy process.

b. To offer members the opportunity to use touch as a means of communication.

Group Application

Twelve members or less. To be used with encounter, personal growth, marathon and t-groups. Best results are obtained if the exercise is used after the members have developed warm, caring feelings for each other.

Application Variables

Time is unlimited, although most exercises will run between fifteen and twenty minutes. The exercise is 70 per cent non-verbal and 30 per cent verbal. A carpeted room which can be darkened is required. Lighted candles will enhance the effect.

Administrative Procedure

a. The facilitator says: "Remove your shoes and socks and lie on the floor in a circle with your feet piled in the middle. Touch the shoulders of the members to your right and left."

b. When all are positioned, he adds: "Take the next (name the number) minutes to relax and sharpen your awareness. Breathe evenly and deeply. Be aware of what you and your body are feeling."

c. After time has expired, he says: "Wriggle and move your feet. Be aware of how it feels to be inundated by other sets of feet. Share with us any fantasies which are occurring within you."

d. After a few minutes (or after all fantasies have been verbalized), he continues: "Communicate by touching shoulders, necks and heads, the feelings you have for one another. Try to be aware of the messages you are receiving. Also, try to be aware of *both* the members who are communicating with you."

e. After a few minutes, he says: "Take hold of your partners' hands. Again communicate your feelings for them to them."

f. After two or three minutes, the facilitator says: "Tell us how you feel right here and now."

g. When responses to step *f* have ceased, the members discuss the experience.

Suggestions for Facilitator Process

Concentrate on the following during processing:

a. Were you able to relax during the exercise? If not, why not? How did your feet feel? Why do you think you placed them in the pile as you did? For example, some of your buried both feet in the middle of the pile, others were on its top, others at the bottom, etc.

b. What touch communication were you receiving? Was your interpretation accurate? How do you explain this? How do you explain your inaccuracy?

c. Were you able to be aware of *both* your partners' messages? If not, why not? If so, how did you accomplish this?

Variations

Variation I

a. Instead of piling feet, have the circle form with members' heads in the middle. All heads should be touching at least two others.
b. Repeat step *b* of the original exercise.
c. Then say: "Use your hands to explore the hands, faces and bodies of other members. Be aware of what you are feeling within you."
d. Repeat steps *e* through *g* of the original exercise.

*EGG TOSS

Subsidiary Goal(s)

a. To allow members the opportunity to be amicably competitive.

Group Application

Twenty members or less. Since dyads are used, group size should be even. Applicable to any group.

Application Variables

Time is unlimited, although most Egg Toss exercises will take between five to ten minutes. The exercise is 100 per cent non-verbal. It should occur outside. If conducted indoors, the room *must not* be carpeted. A supply of eggs equal to the number of dyads is required.

Administrative Procedure

a. The facilitator says: "Let's compete with each other in a friendly, relaxing fashion. Form dyads."
b. When the dyads are formed, the facilitator says: "I will give each dyad an egg. Stand at arms length from each other. When I say go, toss the egg to your partner. He then passes it back."

If you did not break or drop the egg during this exchange, each partner takes *one* step backwards. Repeat the egg toss.

Continue tossing and retreating until we have a winning dyad."

c. After winners have been declared (and the mess cleaned up), the members discuss the experience.

Suggestions for Facilitator Process

Concentrate on the following during processing:

a. *To the winners:* How did you feel about winning? Did you have any egg tossing strategy?
b. *To others:* How do you feel about losing? How did you feel about being first out? How did you feel about being last out?
c. *To all:* Was the competition friendly? How did you feel during the exercise? Did you have fun?

Variations

*Variation I

a. In order to investigate the dynamic of closeness as a factor in competition, have the first dyads form on the closeness and warmth the partners have for each other.
b. Repeat step *b* of the original exercise.
c. Reform dyads based on the distance or neutrality of feelings between the partners.
d. Repeat step *b*.
e. During processing, concentrate on differences in dyadic partners' feelings during the two egg tosses and the effect these differences had on the outcome of the two tosses.

*LOVE TRAIN

Subsidiary Goal(s)

a. To produce an opportunity for creative play.
b. To explore various levels of communication.

Group Application

Any number of members. To be used with any group wishing to utilize an exercise geared toward creative fun and relaxation.

Best results are obtained if the exercise is used after an intense interpersonal session.

Application Variables

Fifteen minutes. The exercise is 80 per cent non-verbal and 20 per cent verbal. The room should be large enough to allow the group unrestrained movement.

Administrative Procedure

a. The facilitator may wish to make some brief comments concerning the importance of playing together as well as working together.

b. He then asks all members to stand up and from a train. Each member should put his hands on the next member's hips.

c. After the train is formed, members should be encouraged to make the appropriate noises and movements associated with trains.

d. While the "train" is moving, the facilitator may wish to ask all members to close their eyes while the first member or the "engine" guides the rest of the group.

e. Although it is not necessary, the members may wish to regroup and discuss the experience.

Suggestions for Facilitator Process

Concentrate on the following during processing:

a. How did it feel to play? Do you feel you actually became part of the train? How did you feel about the rest of the members during the exercise?

b. When you closed your eyes, did you feel comfortable? What types of sounds did you emit? Who was the engine? Why? Which car were you? Why did you choose to be that car?

Variations

None

*PYRAMIDS

Subsidiary Goal(s)

a. To allow members the opportunity to be amicably competitive.

Group Application

Group size is unlimited, although the exercise is most effective when used with twenty members or less. Applicable to any group.

Application Variables

Five minutes. The exercise is 100 per cent non-verbal. A lawn or field are the most ideal locations. If conducted indoors, the room *must* be carpeted, preferably with shag or a thick carpet.

Administrative Procedure[1]

a. The facilitator says: "Let's compete with each other in a friendly, relaxing fashion.

When I say go, I want you to accomplish the following as rapidly as possible. First, form subgroups of six. Second, using your six members, form a human pyramid. Your pyramid will have three at the base, two in the middle and one at the top. Any questions? Go!"

b. After all pyramids are formed, the facilitator declares the winners and says: "All the pyramids should end the exercise by collapsing and falling down. Go ahead, fall."

Suggestions for Facilitator Process

Concentrate on the following during processing:

a. Did you feel competitive? If so, was it friendly or win only competition? Did you enjoy the exercise? If so, why? If not, why not?

b. How did you feel about winning or losing? Did you enjoy collapsing? If so, why? If not, why not?

Variations

None

---

[1]Our Administrative Procedure is based on a group of eighteen. The facilitator should vary the instructions based on the size of his group.

Figure 7-1. Rest

REST

Subsidiary Goal(s)

   a. To explore the dynamics involved in security.

   b. To provide an environment conducive to group cohesion.

   c. To become more aware of one's body.

Group Application

Twelve members or less. To be used with encounter, personal growth, marathon and t-groups. The exercise is designed to provide an environment conducive to total relaxation. It is suggested that the exercise be used after an intense emotional session with groups in which cohesion and warmth have developed.

Application Variables

Fifteen to thirty minutes. The exercise is 100 per cent nonverbal. A darkened room illuminated only by candlelight is recommended.

Administrative Procedure

a. The facilitator presents the following introduction: "We have achieved a sense of unity and peace after much hard work. This exercise is designed to give us an opportunity to rest and relax as a group. Please remove your shoes and socks."

b. After members have removed shoes and socks, the facilitator states: "Everyone lie on the floor. Let's get as close as possible with one another while still remaining comfortable. Please feel free to lie down next to anyone you wish. I would like to suggest that there be no talking."

c. After all members are situated, the facilitator continues: "Close your eyes and listen to the sounds of *Us*. We will rest for (name the time). Relax. Feel the warmth of the group. Feel the security and love which we share with each other."

d. After the time has expired, the facilitator slowly brings the members back. Processing then occurs.

Suggestions for Facilitator Process

Concentrate on the following during processing:

a. What thoughts and feelings did you have during the exercise? Did anyone fall asleep? How relaxed did you become?

b. Did anyone have any fantasies? If so, what? What messages did your body send you? Describe your breathing? What are your present feelings toward the group?

Variations

None

RUNNING THROUGH MY BODY

Subsidiary Goal(s)

a. To explore the dynamics involved in relaxation.

b. To gain greater insight into bodily functions and characteristics.

Group Application

Twelve members or less. To be used with encounter, personal growth, marathon and t-groups.

Application Variables

Forty-five minutes to one hour. The exercise is 100 per cent non-verbal. The room should be large enough to allow members to spread out unrestrained. It is suggested that the room be darkened. Candles may be used to provide minimal lighting.

Administrative Procedure

a. The facilitator asks the members to spread out around the room and to lie down on their backs. All shoes should be removed.

b. Members should have both feet and arms spread out and eyes closed.

c. The facilitator now asks the members to tighten their facial muscles as tightly as possible, then release the tension. The following instructions are then given at five minute intervals.

    1. "I want you to feel your face. Pay close attention to your facial muscles. Try to let your entire face relax completely."

    2. "I now want you to relax your neck. Let your body tensions flow out."

    3. "Let your chest expand. Breathe deeply and let your chest totally relax."

    4. "Now loosen your stomach muscles and try to begin to let your body go."

    5. "Relax your arms and hands. Let your body tensions flow out through your finger tips."

    6. "Let the heaviness of your legs flow out. Relax. Depend completely on the floor to support your weight."

    7. "Relax your feet and toes."

    8. "Now let your entire body float. When you feel ready you may open your eyes and sit up. However, make sure you allow yourself enough time to savor the experience."

d. When all members are ready, the members discuss the experience.

Suggestions for Facilitator Process

Concentrate on the following during processing:

a. What sensations did you experience? What have you learned about your body? Were there any surprises? If so, what?

b. Did you find it difficult to relax? If so, why? Were some parts of your body more difficult to let go of than others? Which ones and why? How do you feel right now?

Variations

Variation I

a. The facilitator may wish to emphasize other parts of the body as well.

b. The same basic procedure as described in the original exercise is then followed.

*SPONTANEOUS UNLOOSENING

Subsidiary Goal(s)

a. To learn to be aware of the body's needs.

b. To learn to "let go" and have fun.

Group Application

Twenty members or less. Applicable to any group. The exercise is quite effective when used near the end of an emotionally charged or highly confrontive session of encounter, personal growth, marathon or t-groups.

Application Variables

Five to ten minutes. The exercise is 100 per cent non-verbal. A carpeted room is needed.

Administrative Procedure

a. Near the end of a session in which members were highly confrontive, emotionally involved, etc., the facilitator says: "Let's do something to help us get rid of some of our tensions."

b. He continues: "Lie on the floor. Close your eyes and concentrate on where in your body your tensions and anxieties are stored and built up.

When you find them, *do* what is needed to get rid of them. Yawn, yell nonsense syllables, scream, roll, jab at the air, pound your chest, and so on. Do, physically and non-verbally, the things that will help you unload and relieve these feelings.

When you feel you are no longer burdened by tension and anxiety, stop. Find another member who has also stopped. Show him non-verbally your positive feelings for him. Then sit down. When we are all finished, we'll discuss this experience."

Suggestions for Facilitator Process

Concentrate on the following during processing:

a. How did you feel before we conducted the exercise? How do you feel now? Why the differences in feeling?

b. What body activities did you engage in? Why? Did they help unloosen your anxiety and tension? If yes, why? If no, why not?

Variations

None

*STILL LIFE

Subsidiary Goal(s)

a. To explore one's creative ability.

b. To enhance group cohesion.

Group Application

Twelve members or less. To be used with encounter, personal growth, marathon and t-groups. Best results are obtained if the exercise is used after a climate of trust has developed within the group.

Application Variables

One hour. The exercise is 100 per cent non-verbal. The room should be large enough to allow members to move about unrestrained.

Administrative Procedure

  a. The facilitator may wish to give a brief lecturette about the value of creative feedback. He then asks for a volunteer.
  b. The volunteer is instructed to create an art piece by using the members within the group. The only stipulation is that there are to be *no* verbal instructions given to the members.
  c. The member creating the art piece must physically move or motion for the members to take the shape he, as the "artist," has in mind for them. By the end of the art piece all members must have been used. If he wishes, other objects within the room may be utilized, (e.g. chairs, flower pots, pillow, etc.).
  d. After the art object has been created, members disassemble and another volunteer is asked for. The same procedure is followed until all members who wish to create an art piece have had the opportunity to do so.

Suggestions for Facilitator Process

Concentrate on the following during processing:

  a. Did you find any value in creating? What types of feedback did you receive from other member's creations? For example, were you always "tacked on," were you always part of the base, and so on?
  b. Did you mind being manipulated as and inanimate object? What have you discovered about yourself?

Variations

None

VIII

SENSORY AWARENESS

THE PRIMARY GOAL for each exercise in this chapter is to help the members become more aware of their various senses and increase their ability to use such senses.

Sensory awareness is a unique entity in the area of group dynamics. There are marathon sessions offered dealing entirely with the expansion of the awareness of senses. There are group dynamics courses which devote a large majority of their classroom time to it. In fact, there are human relations training books which, when describing exercises, appear to consist almost entirely of sensory awareness experiences.

We recognize the fact that *almost all* non-verbal exercises will expose the member, at some level, to sensory awareness. However, we do *not* believe that sensory awareness is the only dynamic one can attain via non-verbal exercises. We have excluded many sensory awareness exercises because we feel that filling this volume entirely with sensory awareness exercises would certainly not meet most facilitator's needs. The fifty-two exercises included should be sufficient.

Relaxation is generally conducive to optimal results in sensory awareness exercises. Therefore, the facilitator should attempt when appropriate, to facilitate an atmosphere conducive to relaxation.

BOUNCE

Subsidiary Goal(s)

    a. To provide an environment conducive to creative play.
    b. To gain greater self-insight.
    c. To release stored up energy.

Group Application

    Twelve members or less. To be used with encounter, personal growth, marathon and t-groups.

Application Variables

Fifteen minutes. The exercise is 100 per cent non-verbal. The room must be large enough to allow the members to spread out without feeling restricted.

Administrative Procedure

a. The facilitator presents the following introduction: "Our body is often a storehouse of untapped energy. Through movement we can often gain many insights into both our feelings and thoughts. I would like you to spread out within the room so that you have ample space to move your body about."

b. After all members have spread out, the facilitator states: "Begin to slowly twist. Let your arms fly through the air. Become aware of the energy being released through your finger tips. Become aware of your breathing. Try and let your entire body flow and move back and forth."

c. After two to three minutes, he adds: "Please stop. Take several deep breaths. Let your body hang loose. Listen to your heart beat. Now touch your chest and feel your heart."

d. After several minutes, he continues: "Begin to bounce. Bounce as high or as low as you wish. Go as fast or as slow as you feel comfortable with. Feel free to bounce around the room. Become aware of the power of your body, legs, arms and chest."

e. After a few minutes, the facilitator states: "Lie down and become aware of you and your body. Get in touch with both your body and your feelings. Close your eyes and relax. Become unified within yourself."

f. After a few minutes, the members discuss the experience.

Suggestions for Facilitator Process

Concentrate on the following during processing:

a. How long has it been since you have tapped into and released your own energy supply? How do you feel? What insights did you gain?

b. What did you become most aware of during the exercise? What part(s) of your body felt most strained? Why?

Variations

None

*CLAY

Subsidiary Goal(s)
a. To achieve group cohesiveness.
b. To examine members' perceptions.
c. To facilitate creativity.
d. To investigate the dynamics of leadership.

Group Application

Twelve members or less. To be used with encounter, personal growth, marathon and t-groups. Best results are obtained if the exercise is used in the latter stages of the group's development.

Application Variables

One hour. The exercise is 100 per cent non-verbal. Fifty to sixty pounds of clay and a piece of plywood large enough to support the clay are required.

Administrative Procedure
a. The facilitator gives the following introduction: "We are going to create a group sculpture out of the clay. We will have one hour in which to non-verbally create such a sculpture. I want you to become aware of where we, as a group, have been and where we are now, and represent that via the clay sculpture. Each member may add to or change the clay in any way he or she feels appropriate. Since we have a large number of people working on the same piece of clay, feel free to scoop out a portion, work on it alone, and then add it to the larger piece."
b. After one hour the group members discuss the experience.

Suggestions for Facilitator Process

Concentrate on the following during processing:
a. What were you aware of in yourself while working on the clay? What did you observe about others as they worked on

the sculpture? Are you satisfied with the sculpture in its final form? If not, why not? How many times did the sculpture change forms? Why?

b. What types of feedback to the group were given via the clay sculpture? Did you work on a small portion or a large portion? Why? Were you aware of the clay itself? That is, its shape, weight, texture, smell, color, warmth, etc? If so, what were you aware of? If not, why not?

c. Who was in charge of the sculpting? How did he (they) earn this position? Why did you let them have it?

Variations

*Variation I

a. Have each member work on a separate sculpture.

b. Then have the members explain the significance and meaning for their sculpture.

c. Then have the group decide which sculpture is "best." Do not define best.

d. During processing concentrate on the members' feelings about having their sculptures judged, how it felt to lose in the competition and how it felt to win.

*Variation II

a. Have the members form dyads with individuals they have distant, neutral, or negative feelings for.

b. The dyads are then to work together, non-verbally, in forming the sculpture.

c. During processing concentrate on any changes in dyadic partner feelings for each other. Explore the reasons for the changes.

*Variation III

a. Have the members form dyads with individuals they have close, positive, warm feelings for.

b. The dyads are then to work together, non-verbally, in forming sculpture.

c. During processing concentrate on any changes in dyadic partner feelings for each other. Explore the reasons for the changes.

*CIRCLES

Subsidiary Goal(s)

a. To provide contact between members.
b. To gain insight into the differences and similarities between members.
c. To explore different forms of non-verbal communication.

Group Application

Twelve members or less. An even number of participants is required. To be used with encounter, personal growth, marathon and t-groups. The exercise is especially effective when used as an introduction to physical contact with beginning groups whose members are hesitant to touch each other.

Application Variables

Fifteen minutes. The exercise is 100 per cent non-verbal.

Administrative Procedure

a. The facilitator asks that the group form two circles, one within the other. There should be an equal number of members in each circle.
b. When the circles are formed, he says: "The inner circle members are to face the outer circle members. Each of you should be facing *one* member of the outer circle.

Both circle members are to maintain eye contact with the person being faced. Also, place your arms on each other's shoulders. All of this is to be done non-verbally."
c. After two or three minutes, the facilitator tells the outer circle members: "Move to the right so that you face the inner circle member to the immediate left of your last inner circle partner. The inner circle is to remain stationary."
d. When the new positions are established, the facilitator says: "Maintaining eye contact, reach out and touch each other's face."
e. After two or three minutes, the facilitator tells the outer circle to rotate as before.

Figures 8-1. Circles

f. When this has been done, he adds: "Touch one another's sides, just below the rib cage."

g. After two or three minutes, the facilitator has the outer circle rotate and then has the members "touch each other's hips."

h. After two or three minutes, the facilitator stops the exercise and has the members discuss it.

Suggestions for Facilitator Process

Concentrate on the following during processing:

a. How do you feel about the experience? Did any one mem-

Figures 8-2. Circles

ber's touch mean more to you than the others? Why? How did you feel about being touched? About touching?
b. Which touching stage was most gratifying? Why? Which was least satisfying? Why? What have you learned about yourself? About other members?

Variations

Variation I
a. Use the same procedure as described in the original exercise.
b. However, vary the body areas touched. The areas touched will depend upon the level of rapport, trust and care of the group.

Figures 8-3. Circles

*CLOUDS

Subsidiary Goal(s)

    a. To form group cohesion.

    b. To explore the dynamics involved in close physical contact.

    c. To experience the process of creativity.

    d. To explore member use of fantasy.

Group Application

    Twelve members or less. To be used with encounter, personal growth, marathon and t-groups. Best results are obtained if the exercise is used after the group has had ample sessions for some feelings of group unity to have developed.

Application Variables

Thirty minutes. The exercise is 100 per cent non-verbal. The room must be large enough to allow members unrestrained movement.

Administrative Procedure

a. The facilitator gives the following instructions to the entire group: "I would like you to assume a comfortable position while maintaining a circle and close your eyes. Get in touch with your own body. Pay attention to your neck, stomach, legs, and arms."

b. After several minutes, he says: "Very slowly, reach out with your arms and hands until you are touching the members on both sides of you. Please do not open your eyes. I want you to imagine that you are a small particle of matter coming together with other particles to form a cloud."

c. After all members have made physical contact, the facilitator continues: "Without breaking any physical contact, I would like you all to stand and begin to slowly make the circle smaller. Imagine that the wind is gently blowing all of us through the sky. Feel free to sway with the wind as we come together."

d. After several minutes the facilitator says: "I would like you to become aware of your own body, the feelings of closeness which you may have, and your reactions to the physical contact in which you are engaged. Explore yourself. Let your entire being feel the freedom, the lightness, and the warmth."

e. When the facilitator feels that the group has reached a point of maximizing the experience, he states: "Slowly come apart. Take your own time in dissassociating yourself from the experience. When we are all ready we will come together to discuss the experience."

Suggestions for Facilitator Process

Concentrate on the following during processing:

a. What feelings and thoughts were you aware of when you first started the exercise? What type of feelings did you have when I asked you to reach out and touch the members seated next to you?

b. What were you aware of when the circle began to come closer? Did you actually feel as though you were floating in the wind? If so, what did your body experience? Do you feel closer to the other members? Why? Why not?

Variations

*Variation I

a. Steps *a* through *d* of the original exercise are repeated.

b. The facilitator then says: "Break up into smaller clouds composed of two or more people."

c. When the smaller cloud groups have been formed, he says: "Now, float. If you make contact with other clouds, decide whether your cloud wishes to bounce off them or absorb them."

d. When the facilitator feels the group has maximized the experience, he has the members regroup and discuss it. Processing should concentrate on why the members chose their cloud partners, why they decided to merge or repel, and how they felt about the other clouds.

*Variation II

a. Variation I is repeated. However, step *b* is changed to: "Break up into small clouds composed of two or more people. Choose your cloud partners based on how distant, neutral, or negative your feelings for them are. *Do not* form a cloud with someone you feel quite close to."

b. The exercise continues as in Variation I.

c. Processing should concentrate on why the cloud partners chose each other and how and why their feelings for each other have changed.

*Variation III

a. Variation I is repeated. However step *b* is changed to: "Break up into small clouds composed of two or more people. Choose your cloud partners based on how close, positive, or loving your feelings for them are. Choose someone you really *care* about."

b. The exercise continues as in Variation I.

c. Processing should concentrate on why the cloud partners chose each other and how and why their feelings for each other have changed.

CONVERSATIONS

Subsidiary Goal(s)

a. To gain insight into the self-concept of oneself and others.

b. To explore the process of fantasy.

c. To gain insight into bodily functions.

Group Application

Twelve members or less. To be used only with encounter, personal growth, marathon and t-groups.

Application Variables

Fifteen to twenty minutes. The exercise is 100 per cent non-verbal.

Administrative Procedure

a. The facilitator asks the members to sit comfortably, with their eyes closed.

b. The following statement is then made: "I want you to relax. Breathe deeply and let the tensions flow out through your body. Let your neck, shoulders and arms relax. Let the weight of your body be completely supported by the floor."

c. When the facilitator feels that all members have reached a point of relaxation, the following instructions are given: "Place your hands together. I want you not *only* to touch, but to feel your hands. Get to know your hands, their shape, texture, temperature, etc."

d. After several minutes, the facilitator says: "I want you to carry on a silent conversation between your hands. Let your left hand know what your right hand is feeling and vice-versa.

e. After several minutes, the facilitator adds: "Discuss, by using your hands, the differences and similarities between them. When you are finished, let your hands say goodbye to each other and open your eyes."

f. When all members have opened their eyes, the group members discuss the experience.

Suggestions for Facilitator Process

Concentrate on the following during processing:

a. What have you learned about your hands? Were there any surprises? If so, what and why? How did you initially feel about having your hands talk to one another? How do you now feel about it?

b. What differences and similarities did you discover between your hands? What were your hand feelings toward one another?

Variations

Variation I

a. Repeat steps *a* through *e* of the original exercise.

b. Have members introduce their hands to other members and carry on conversations the respective members have for each other.

c. During processing concentrate on the differences in the hand conversations when conducted with oneself as opposed to with another member.

*DEVELOPING SELF AND OTHER AWARENESS

Subsidiary Goal(s)

a. To learn to carefully perceive another person.

b. To develop general body awareness.

Group Application

Twelve members or less. Since dyads are used, the group size should be even. If at all possible, the group composition should be even by sexes, as mixed dyads appear to be the most dynamic. Applicable to any group. Is most effective when used with classroom and t-groups when body, self, or other person awareness is a matter of concern.

Application Variables

Ten to fifteen minutes for the individual awareness phase (see steps *a* through *e* and ten to fifteen minutes for the dyadic phase (see steps *f through j*). The exercise is 70 per cent nonverbal and 30 per cent verbal. The room must be large enough to allow the dyads some feeling of privacy.

Administrative Procedure

a. The facilitator tells the members to spread out around the room and find a spot that feels comfortable.

b. He then says: "Sit quietly. Close your eyes. Try to relax. Breathe evenly and deeply and concentrate on the feeling of being wholly and entirely yourself. Try to be as aware of yourself as you can."

c. After a minute or two he continues: "Try to feel each and every part of your body. Be aware of your head, scalp, eyes, eye muscles, and neck. Move all around your body. Be aware of the feelings in your stomach, chest, thighs, legs, calves and feet.

Where are you tense? Go to that spot and find the why for the tenseness. Where are you relaxed? Go there and feel the calming effect such relaxed areas exude.

Go into your body and find that spot which is your center, that place around which all of you is balanced."

d. After five minutes, he continues: "Become more aware of incoming sensations. What feelings, sensations, and stimuli are your eyes, ears, nose, and touch aware of?"

e. After two or three minutes, the facilitator says: "Find another person and form a dyad." When this is accomplished, he continues: "Share with each other some of the feelings and experiences you have just had."

f. After three to five minutes, the facilitator says: "Form dyads. You may stay with your current partner or find another. When you have done this, sit quietly and face each other."

g. When the dyads are formed and seated, the facilitator says: "Silently study and examine your partner. See and be aware of his face, posture, and body composition. Notice his hands, legs, and expressions. Look at his eyes and try to get into him."

h. After two or three minutes, he says: "Close your eyes. Try to recall the who and what of your partner. Remember his voice and his body and face expressions. Fantasize what it would be like to touch him and be touched by him."

i. After two or three minutes, he says: "Open your eyes. Communicate non-verbally with your partner. Try to tell him how you feel about him. Let him know where he is with you."

j. After two or three minutes, the facilitator continues: "Share verbally with each other the feelings and experiences you have had during your dyadic encounter."

k. After five minutes, the facilitator may end the exercise and process it or he may have dyads form and repeat steps *f* through *j*.

Suggestions for Facilitator Process

Concentrate on the following during processing:

a. Share with us some of the feelings you had when you were by yourself concentrating on yourself. Which areas were tense and tight? Why? Where were you relaxed? Why? Where was the center of your being? Why there?

b. What feelings did you have during the dyadic phase? What awarenesses about your partner were present? What kinds of verbal reactions did you share?

c. When told to communicate non-verbally, how did you feel? Who touched each other? Why? Who did not touch? Why?

d. Which was most satisfying, self-awareness of self-exploration or other-awareness and exploration? Why?

Variations

None

*DID I MAKE THIS?

Subsidiary Goal(s)

a. To explore the creative process.
b. To create a playful environment.
c. To explore the dynamics involved in self-feedback.
d. To gain greater insight into members' resources.

Group Application

Twelve members or less. To be used with any group concerned with the exploration of sensory awareness.

Application Variables

Forty-five minutes. The exercise is 100 per cent non-verbal. One blindfold and five pounds of clay are required for each member. A piece of plywood or cardboard is recommended for each member. This provides a working surface for the clay. The room must be large enough to allow members to spread out without feeling unduly restricted.

Administrative Procedure

a. The facilitator may wish to give the following introduction: "Most of us rely on our vision when creating. We are going to try to create without using our vision. Instead we will rely solely on touch. I am going to ask you to spread out within the room and to find a semi-private spot."
b. After all members have found a spot within the room, the facilitator passes out five pounds of clay to each member along with a blindfold and a piece of material on which the clay can be supported.
c. The facilitator then says: "Set up your clay and proceed to put on your blindfold. For the next thirty minutes I want you to create, either symbolically or descriptivly, a sculpture which represents you. There is to be no talking or peeking. Depend on touch alone to create. Please begin." (Since the

clay should be wet enough to work with, it should be soften-
ed and saturated. If not, place a cup of water by each member).

   d. After thirty minutes, the facilitator asks the members to remove their blindfolds. He says: "Non-verbally, explore the
creations you and the others made."

   e. After all creations have been examined, the members discuss
the experience.

Suggestions for Facilitator Process

Concentrate on the following during processing:

   a. What was your first reaction when you saw your creation?
Did it surprise you? If so, why? Do you feel that you accomplished what you had in mind?

   b. What were your thoughts, feelings and reactions as you examined the other sculptures? How did you decide to represent you through your sculpture? What insights have you
gained about yourself?

Variations

None

*ENVIRONMENT

Subsidiary Goal(s)

   a. To explore the dynamics involved in creativity.
   b. To increase listening skills.
   c. To examine the role projection plays in our listening.

Group Application

Twelve members or less. To be used with encounter, personal
growth, marathon and t-groups. Best results are obtained if the
exercise is used with members who have had exposure to sensory awareness.

Application Variables

Forty-five minutes. The exercise is 70 per cent non-verbal and
30 per cent written. Pencils and paper are required. The ex-

ercise is designed to take place outdoors. The ideal location is open space.

Administrative Procedure

a. The facilitator asks that the entire group meet outside. Pencils and papers are passed around to each member.

b. The following instructions are given: "The exercise we are about to engage in is designed to help us become more aware of our surroundings. Each member is to go explore on his own. As you explore, try to listen to the environment. There are many different levels at which we may listen. I would like you to write down the object(s) you are listening to and then write down what they are saying. For example, I may be listening to the wind. It may be saying, 'Come out and breathe me. Let me move you.' You will have forty-five minutes to explore. When the time has elapsed, we will regroup and share what we have heard. Do not explore together. Do not talk to any other member. Please begin."

c. After forty-five minutes the members regroup and share their listening perceptions.

Suggestions for Facilitator Process

Concentrate on the following during processing:

a. What did you hear? Were you surprised at what the objects were saying to you? What place did projection play in what you heard the objects say to you? How did this type of listening differ from the way you normally listen?

b. Did you become more aware of your surroundings? If so, in what way? How do you feel about what the other members listened to? Any similarities?

Variations

None

EYE MILL

Subsidiary Goal(s)

a To gain greater insight into the dynamics involved in nonverbal communication.

b. To give and receive feedback.

c. To explore the dynamics involved in eye contact.

Group Application

Twelve members or less. To be used with any group concerned with open, honest communication.

Application Variables

Ten minutes. The exercise is 100 per cent non-verbal. The room must be large enough to allow members unrestrained movement.

Administrative Procedure

a. The facilitator may wish to give a brief talk on the importance and value of eye contact.

b. He then asks all members to rise.

c. The following instructions are given: "I would like all of you to walk around in a close circle and look each other directly in the eyes. Do not pause in any spot for more than a few moments. I will tell you when to stop. Remember there is to be absolutely no talking. Please begin."

d. After ten minutes the facilitator should ask the group to stop and discuss the experience.

Suggestions for Facilitator Process

Concentrate on the following during processing:

a. What feelings did you have as you walked around? Was it difficult for you to look at another member? Who and why? What messages were you sending?

b. What messages were you receiving? Did you have any physical contact? Why? Why not? Was it difficult not to pause? Why? What have you learned about yourself from this experience? About others?

Variations

None

EXPAND

Subsidiary Goal(s)

a. To explore the dynamics involved in fantasy.

b. To gain insight into the process of relaxation.

Group Application

Twelve members or less. To be used with encounter, personal growth, marathon and t-groups. Best results are obtained if the exercise is used with members who have had some previous exposure to sensory awareness.

Application Variables

Fifteen minutes. The exercise is 100 per cent non-verbal. The room must be large enough to allow members to spread out without feeling unduly restricted.

Administrative Procedure

a. The facilitator tells the members to spread out within the room and to lie on their backs with their eyes closed.

b. The facilitator then gives the following instructions: "I want you to breathe evenly and deeply. Let your body float. Don't try to control it. Sense how wide you actually are. As you breathe pretend that your chest is a cavern. As you take in the air let yourself expand."

c. After several minutes, the facilitator adds: "Begin to let your entire body expand. Stretch your legs and arms. Become aware of the space you are occupying and the space within you. Let yourself expand as far as possible."

d. After several more minutes, he continues: "Start closing your space. Bring your arms and legs closer to your body. Become aware of the messages your body is sending to you. When you feel that you have *closed* yourself, slowly begin to dissassociate yourself from the experience. When you feel ready, join the circle for processing."

Suggestions for Facilitator Process

Concentrate on the following during processing:

a. What feelings did you have during the experience? What were you aware of? What did you learn about your own body?

b. How did it feel when you "expanded" yourself? What differences did you discover between "expanding" and "closing" yourself? Did your breathing differ? If so, in what way?

Variations

None

*FACES

Subsidiary Goal(s)

a. To give and receive feedback.
b. To explore the dynamics involved in perception.
c. To achieve closer interpersonal contact.
d. To explore differences between sexes.

Group Application

Twelve members or less. Since dyads are used, group size should be even. To be used with encounter, personal growth, marathon and t-groups. Best results are achieved if the group has an equal number of males and females.

Application Variables

Thirty minutes. The exercise is 100 per cent non-verbal. The room must be large enough to allow members to move about unrestricted.

Administrative Procedure

a. The facilitator asks members to non-verbally form male-female dyads.

b. The following instructions are given: "Find two other dyads and join them. I would like the women in the subgroup to sit down with their backs toward the center of the circle and with their eyes closed. The men are to stand up and silently move around the circle and sit down in front of any female member *except* your original partner."

c. After this is completed the facilitator adds: "I want the men to study the face of the member you sat down in front of. Study the texture, shape, color and other features of your partner's face. When you feel you've reached a point of experiencing your partner's face, gently explore it by touch."

d. After several minutes the facilitator adds: "Let your partner know when you have finished. Then take a few minutes to discuss the experience."

e. The same basic procedure is then repeated, with the men sitting on the inside of the circle and the woman on the outside.

f. When the exercise is completed, the members discuss the experience.

Suggestions for Facilitator Process

Concentrate on the following during processing:

a. *To members on the outside of circle:* What did you notice about your partner's face? How did you decide which member to sit in front of? What did you experience when touching your partner's face?

b. *To members on the inside of circle:* How did you feel not knowing who was in front of you studying your face? How did you feel when your partner touched your face? What were you aware of during the experience, both psychologically and physiologically?

Variations

Variation I

a. Have members intentionally pair off with members of the same sex.

b. The original Administrative Procedure is then utilized.

FLOWERS

Subsidiary Goal(s)

a. To explore the process of creativity.

Figure 8-4. Flowers

    b. To experience physical and emotional growth.
    c. To experience the process of fantasy.

Group Application

Twelve members or less. To be used only with encounter, personal growth, marathon and t-groups. Best results are obtained if the exercise is used in the advanced stage of the group's life.

Figure 8-5. Flowers

Application Variables

Twenty minutes. The exercise is 100 per cent non-verbal. The room must be large enough to allow members unrestrained movement.

Figures 8-6. Flowers

Administrative Procedure

    a. The facilitator asks members to spread out within the room. The following introduction is then given: "The process of growth is a beautiful experience. In many ways it is analogous to the bud of a flower. We bloom and flourish, although many times we tend to wither. I would like you to lie on your back and become in touch with your own growing and

Figure 8-7. Flowers

withdrawing or withering process. Breathe deeply and let your body relax while your thoughts and feelings flow."

b. After several minutes, the facilitator continues: "I want you to assume a position of withdrawal. Close your body. You may wish to put your head between your legs or assume a fetal position. Get in close touch with your feeling of withdrawal."

c. After a few minutes, he adds: "When you feel ready, I want you to physically and emotionally experience your growth.

Begin to open and spread your body out. Bloom! Do this slowly and become aware of what your body is doing as you go through this change. After you have spread as fully as you feel, take some time to become aware of your thoughts and feelings about the experience."

d. After the facilitator feels that all members have completed the experience, the members discuss it.

Suggestions for Facilitator Process

Concentrate on the following during processing:

a. What did the experience mean for you? What was your body doing while you withdrew? While you opened?

b. Did you actually experience your own growth? After you physically opened up, what were your thoughts and feelings? What have you learned about yourself?

Variations

None

*FOOD AWARENESS

Subsidiary Goal(s)

a. To help members become more in touch with their feelings.

b. To provide an opportunity for creative play.

Group Application

Twelve members or less. To be used with encounter, personal growth, marathon and t-groups.

Application Variables

Fifteen to twenty minutes. The exercise is 100 per cent non-verbal. One apple or other type of fruit for each member is required.

Administrative Procedure

a. The facilitator says: "Often when we eat we completely ignore the food which we are eating. We tend to forget that food has weight, shape, texture, temperature and smell. Close your eyes. I am going to pass around a piece of fruit to each one of you. Take the next ten minutes to explore your piece of fruit without biting into it. Explore your fruit in any conceivable manner you can think of. Keep your eyes closed. Please begin."

b. After ten minutes, the facilitator states: "Please keep your eyes closed. Begin to eat your piece of fruit. Slowly savor each bite. Again explore the fruit while you are eating it."

c. After the members have finished eating their fruit, the facilitator adds: "Before you open your eyes, explore the remainder of your fruit. After you feel you have completely explored your fruit to its fullest potential, open your eyes and examine it."

d. Several minutes after the members have opened their eyes, the group rejoins for processing.

Suggestions for Facilitator Process

Concentrate on the following during processing:

a. What were you aware of while exploring your piece of fruit? Did you gain any new insights? If so, what? In what ways did you explore your fruit?

b. Did you have any personal or sensual feelings toward your fruit? What did you feel as you bit into the fruit? What have you learned about food? About yourself?

Variations

Variation I

a. Have members pair off into dyads.

b. Each dyad is given one piece of fruit.

c. The facilitator states: "Close your eyes. Non-verbally explore your piece of fruit together. Help your partner share any discoveries you have made."

d. After ten minutes the dyads are told to eat the fruit.

e. Steps *c* and *d* of the original exercise are then administered.

*FRUIT, LIKE PEOPLE, ARE DIFFERENT

Subsidiary Goal(s)

a. To learn to pay attention to detail.
b. To help one be aware of individual differences.
c. To learn the role projection plays in attributing personal characteristics to inanimate objects.

Group Application

Twelve members or less. If the exercise is used with more than twelve members, the facilitator may wish to use subgroups of four to seven. Applicable to any group, but most frequently used with encounter, personal growth, marathon and t-groups.

Application Variables

Twenty-five to thirty-five minutes. The exercise is 60 per cent non-verbal and 40 per cent verbal. A bag containing a number of fruit equivalent to the group size is needed. If there are twelve members, the facilitator would place twelve of *one* fruit in the bag. We recommend using oranges, limes, lemons, grapefruit, pears, plums, or peaches. In the Administrative Procedure section we will use peaches for the fruit objects.

Administrative Procedure

a. Prior to the group session, the facilitator fills a bag with a number of peaches equal to the number of members. For example with ten members the bag would contain ten peaches.
b. When the group convenes, the facilitator says: "Non-verbally, each of you go to the bag and take a peach. Then go back and sit down."
c. When all members have finished, he says: "During the next five minutes study your peach very, very *carefully*. Try to get to know it as *completely* as it can be known. Touch it, feel it, see it, taste its skin. Do *not* bite it! Hear the sound it makes. Try to *be* the peach. Become so aware of your peach that you will know it anywhere."
d. After five minutes, the facilitator continues: "Tell us about your peach. Tell us its name. Tell us its likes and dislikes.

Tell us what makes it different and special."

e. When all members are finished, the facilitator collects the peaches and places them in the bag. He shakes it to insure that the peaches are mixed thoroughiy.

f. He empties the bag on the floor and says: "Each of you is to find his own peach. Do this one at a time."

g. When everyone has completed step *f*, the facilitator processes the experience.

Suggestions for Facilitator Process

Concentrate on the following during processing:

a. Is there anyone who did not find his own peach? Seldom are there any yesses. If there are, ask why and tell the person(s) to go find the correct peach. Almost always, each person will have correctly identified his own peach. Ask why? Pursue the dynamics involved. Make the members aware of really how different one peach is from all others. Relate this learning to labeling and sterotyping.

b. Who went first to discover his peach? Why? Who went second and third? Why? Who were the last three? Why?

c. What have you learned from this experience? How does this learning relate to our group? How does it relate to life? What role did projection play in your fruit names and description?

Variations

*Variation I

a. Instead of fruit, the facilitator can use inanimate objects which appear the same. For example, nuts, bolts, can openers, pieces of paper, etc. can be used.

b. The exercise is then conducted as above.

*GROUP MASSAGE[1]

Subsidiary Goal(s)

a. To learn to give and receive care and tenderness.

b. To achieve a peak experience.

---

[1]Adapted from an exercise designed by Judy Morris, Counselor, West Intermediate School, Mt. Pleasant, Michigan.

   c. To learn how one reacts to a bombardment of tactile sensations.

Group Application

Any size group which can be divided into subgroups of six. To be used with encounter, personal growth, marathon and t-groups whose members have developed feelings of warmth and care.

Application Variables

One to one and a half hours. The exercise is 100 per cent non-verbal. The room should be large enough to allow the subgroups to spread out without feeling unduly restricted. An ample supply of massage oil or hand/body lotion is needed. A room lighted only by candles will enhance the effect.

Administrative Procedure

   a. The facilitator asks that subgroups of six be formed. They are told to spread out within the room. (Shoes, socks and any unnecessary clothing is to be removed.)

   b. He then explains that the group massage experience will involve trust and learning to let go of one's feelings of tightness so that the member can become more aware of himself, his tenderness, and his feelings about showing and receiving care.

He adds that every member will be massaged by the five others in the subgroup. Each will be massaged for an equal period of time. (Five to fifteen minutes) . The oil or cream is then placed in positions accessible to all members.

   c. The facilitator continues: "One member is to lie down. He will be massaged by you. Each of you should take the head, a hand, or a foot. Massage positions are to be switched as each person is massaged.

The important thing to remember is that you should try to show care and tenderness through your touch.

The person being massaged should close his eyes and try to

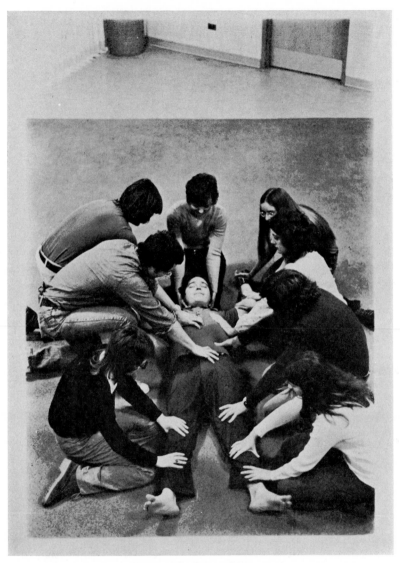

Figure 8-8. Group Massage

let his tightness flow out, relax, and enjoy the massage and the numerous tactile sensations it is creating."

d. The facilitator should notify members when it is time to

switch positions. Time may be allowed for processing after each massage. However, processing after everyone has been massaged is equally beneficial and is recommended.

Suggestions for Facilitator Process

Concentrate on the following during processing:

a. *To massaged members:* What were your feelings as you were being massaged? Did you feel uncomfortable at any time? When? How did you cope with this feeling? Did you feel the massagers were tender and caring? How did it feel to be massaged in so many places at one time?

b. *To massagers:* How did it feel to massage a person's head? His foot? His hand? What differences did you note between the different massage areas? What were your thoughts and feelings as you massaged the member? How did you try to show your care and tenderness?

c. *To all:* Were you more comfortable giving or receiving a massage? Why? What have you learned about yourself and other members?

Variations

None

*HAND LOTION

Subsidiary Goal(s)

a. To learn to communicate feelings through touch.
b. To help develop group unity and feelings of closeness.

Group Application

Twelve members or less. To be used with encounter, personal growth, marathon and t-groups whose members have developed warmth, care and trust between each other.

Application Variables

Twenty to thirty minutes. The exercise is 100 per cent non-verbal. A bottle of hand lotion is required.

Administrative Procedure

a. The facilitator asks that the members sit on the floor in a circle. He then says: "Hold the hands of the members to your right and left. Close your eyes and get in touch with their hands. Try to be aware of the feelings and vibrations *each* partner is sending to you.

b. After a few minutes, he continues: "I am now going to place some hand lotion between each set of hands." He then does so.

c. After all have been given a quantity of lotion, the facilitator says: "Work the hand lotion into each others' hands. As you do this, try to be aware of the feeling the lotion has. Be aware of how its presence affects the texture of your hands. At the same time, explore your partners' hands. Be aware of the similarities and differences between their hands."

d. After four or five minutes, he says: "Explore your partners' fingers."

e. After a few minutes, the facilitator says: "I will now ask you to communicate some specific feelings to your partners. As you do this, be aware of *each* of the messages you are receiving. Try to become aware of the differences between the two partners' means of communicating with you."

f. At one minute intervals, the facilitator says the following:

 1. "Communicate concern."
 2. "Communicate neutrality."
 3. "Communicate warmth."
 4. "Communicate anger."
 5. "Communicate tenderness."

g. After instruction 5, the facilitator says: "Now communicate your here and now feelings for your partners. When you are ready, stop and rejoin the original circle."

Suggestions for Facilitator Process

Concentrate on the following during processing:

a. Tell us how your hand sensations differed between step one,

when you had no lotion, and step two, when you did have
lotion.
b. What did you discover about yourself? What did you learn
about your partners? What feelings and reactions did you
have as you rubbed the lotion in and explored your partners'
hands?
c. Were you able to become aware of *each* of your partners? If
no, why not? Did your partners have different ways of communicating during the feeling phase? If so, how did they
differ? Which feeling was most easily sent and received?
Which feeling was most difficult to send and receive?

Variations

*Variation I
a. Establish subgroups of three or more based on the distance
or neutrality the members feel for each other.
b. Repeat steps *a* through *g* of the original exercise.
c. During processing, concentrate on any changes between the
feelings the subgroup partners had for each other. Explore
the reasons for the changes in feelings.

*HANDS

Subsidiary Goal(s)

a. To gain greater insight into the differences and similarities
between group members.
b. To explore different levels of communication.
c. To gain insight into one's feelings about physical contact.

Group Application

Twelve members or less. Since dyads are used, group size should
be even. To be used with any group concerned with expanding
sensory awareness.

Application Variables

Twenty minutes. The exercise is 100 per cent non-verbal. The
room should be large enough to allow members unrestrained
movement.

Administrative Procedure

   a. The facilitator asks members to mill around non-verbally and to form dyads. Each dyad is told to go to a separate corner of the room.
   b. The members are asked to sit down and face one another. The following instructions are then given: "I would like you to close your eyes and take hold of one another's hands. First of all I want you to feel and explore your partner's hands. Pay close attention to skin texture, shape, and warmth."
   c. After five minutes, the facilitator asks all members to express their feelings for and about one another by use of their hands only.
   d. After three minutes, the members are told to open their eyes and non-verbally invite another dyad to join them.
   e. The four members are to sit with their eyes closed. Each member is told: "Introduce your partner's hands to the two new members in your quartet."
   f. After ten minutes, the members discuss the experience.

Suggestions for Facilitator Process

   Concentrate on the following during processing:
   a. *To the original dyads:* What types of dynamics, thoughts and feelings were you aware of when touching your partner? What feelings did you express? What feelings did you receive? How does this level of communication differ from verbal communication?
   b. *To the four member groups:* In what way did you introduce your partner? Do you feel your introduction was perceived accurately? How did you feel when being introduced?

Variations

   None

HANDSHAKE

Subsidiary Goal(s)

   a. To give and receive feedback.
   b. To provide an environment conducive to creative play.

c. To examine members' perceptions.

Group Application

Twelve members or less. To be used with encounter, personal growth, marathon and t-groups. The exercise may derive its greatest benefits by utilizing it once in the initial stage of the group's development and once in the latter stage of the group's life.

Application Variables

Ten to fifteen minutes. The exercise is 100 per cent non-verbal. The room must be large enough to allow the members unrestricted movement.

Administrative Procedure

a. The facilitator may wish to give the following introduction: "Most of us are use to going through the everyday formality of shaking hands. Seldom do we give much thought to the other person's hand as we shake it. For the next few minutes I am going to ask you to non-verbally mill around and shake hands with other members. Pay attention to the warmth, shape, texture and grip of the other members' hands as well as your own. Cue in on the feedback being given to you and sent from you. Please begin."

b. After several minutes, the facilitator adds: "I now want you to use the opposite hand to shake hands. Please repeat the same procedure as before."

c. After all members have shaken hands, they discuss the experience.

Suggestions for Facilitator Process

Concentrate on the following during processing:

a. What impressions did you receive from your handshakes? What were you aware of during the exercise? What messages was your body sending to you?

b. When you reversed hands what differences did you discover? Have you gained any new insights about yourself or other members? What are they? How did you gain them?

Variations

*Variation I
a. Have the members create new methods of "shaking hands" e.g. shaking feet, elbows, heads, backs, legs, etc.
b. They are then to non-verbally make contact by using these modes of touch.

*HOME

Subsidiary Goal(s)

a. To gain greater insight into spatial relationships.
b. To explore physical surroundings.
c. To explore the relationship between perception and space.

Group Application

Twelve members or less. Applicable to any group, but most frequently used with encounter, personal growth, marathon and t-groups. Best results are obtained if the exercise is used with a group that has met for a period of time in the same room.

Application Variables

Thirty minutes. The exercise is 50 per cent verbal and 50 per cent non-verbal.

Administrative Procedure

a. The facilitator makes the following statement: "I would like all of us to silently think about the physical space we are occupying in the group. If you have consistently remained in one spot, I would like you to become more aware of why you feel comfortable in that particular space."
b. After several minutes, the facilitator adds: "I want you all to look around the room and find a spot which you feel is most *unlike* your own. When you have found that spot, I would like you to go over and sit there."
c. After all members have occupied their new spaces, the facilitator asks them to discuss their feelings about the new space,

as well as the differences and similarities between it and their previous locale.

d. After all members have had an opportunity to discuss their new space, the facilitator says: "Return to your original space. Get in touch with how it now feels. See if it alters any of your perceptions about the room or the members in it."

e. The members then discuss the experience.

Suggestions for Facilitator Process

Concentrate on the following during processing:

a. How did you choose the space unlike your original one? What differences did you discover? Did it alter any of your perceptions?

b. How do you now feel about your original space? Do you feel sitting next to different members has any impact on your feelings for them? If so, in what way?

Variations

None

*HOT AND COLD

Subsidiary Goal(s)

a. To help one realize how inattentive he usually is when using his senses.

Group Application

Twelve members or less. Applicable to any group.

Application Variables

Twenty to thirty minutes. The exercise is 100 per cent non-verbal. Drinking glasses, tea cups, instant tea mix, spoons, napkins and ice are required. (Any other beverages which may be served hot and/or cold may be substituted for tea. See *Variation 1*).

Administrative Procedure

a. The facilitator says: "Let's take the opportunity to sharpen our senses and to learn how little we use their potential."

b. He then says: "Please go to the table and make yourself a cup of hot tea." (The water *must* be boiling hot.)

c. When all have done so and are reseated, he says the following at one or two minute intervals:

    1. "Stir your tea. As you do so, be aware of the sound. Hear the tea moving. Hear the spoon and the cup as they make contact. Listen!"

    2. "Look at your tea. Really look! Notice the color, the sparkle, the movement."

    3. "Hold your cup. Cradle it in two hands. Feel the warmth of the cup. Really feel the tea cup."

    4. "Smell your tea. Try to notice how the smell moves and varies."

d. He then says: "Drink your tea. Drink it slowly. Savor its taste. Roll it around in your mouth. Really *taste* it."

e. After all have finished, the facilitator says: "Go fix yourself a glass of iced tea."

f. When all have done so and sat down, he repeats the statements in step *c,* using the words glass for cup and cold for warmth.

g. Step *d* is repeated.

Suggestions for Facilitator Process

Concentrate on the following during processing:

a. How has your sensory awareness benefited from today's experience? Which sense(s) seemed to improve the most? How and why?

b. Which was most pleasing to your sense of (name the sense), hot or cold tea? Why?

Variations

*Variation I

a. Any *one* beverage which can be served hot (or warm or luke-warm) *and* cold can be used. For example:

hot coffee	vs	iced coffee
warm milk	vs	ice milk
warm pop	vs.	ice cold pop
warm beer	vs.	ice cold beer

It is important that the *same* beverage be used. This helps in the sensory evaluation, for the taste is similar yet entirely different.

INSIDE–OUTSIDE

Subsidiary Goal(s)

a. To gain greater insight into reality.
b. To increase listening skills.
c. To gain greater awareness of the process of avoidance.

Group Application

Twelve members or less. Since dyads are used, group size should be even. To be used with encounter, personal growth, marathon and t-groups. Best results are obtained if the exercise is used in the latter stage of development of the group's life.

Application Variables

Forty-five minutes. The exercise is 60 per cent non-verbal and 40 per cent verbal. The room must be large enough to allow members to spread out without feeling unduly restrained. A darkened room lighted only by candles may be used to enhance the atmosphere.

Administrative Procedure

a. The facilitator asks members to non-verbally mill around and to form dyads.
b. The facilitator then gives the following instructions: "I would like the dyad members to sit down and face one another. Keep your eyes open. I want you to look at one another and become aware of what you see. Notice your partner's eyes, hair, lips, arms, etc."
c. After several minutes, the facilitator adds: "Now close your eyes and become aware of what you are experiencing within you."
d. The facilitator now states: "I want you to notice if what you are feeling is pleasant or unpleasant. Try and get in touch

with how you differentiate between pleasant and unpleasant experiences."

e. After several minutes, he continues: "I would like you to try and search yourself. Silently become aware of any feelings or thoughts which you have been avoiding since we began the exercise. When you have gotten a handle on these avoided feelings, I want you to respond to them in any way you deem appropriate.

After you have responded to your feelings, open your eyes."

f. After all members have opened their eyes, the facilitator tells the dyadic partners to discuss with each other their experiences.

g. After fifteen minutes, the members discuss the experience.

Suggestions for Facilitator Process

Concentrate on the following during processing:

a. What were you aware of as you looked at your partner? How were you feeling during that time? What type of images did you receive when you closed your eyes?

b. How did your awareness differ when you were concentrating on another member versus when you were concentrating on yourself? How did you differentiate between pleasant and unpleasant experiences? Were you avoiding any thoughts or feelings? If so, what and why?

c. How did you respond to your feelings? What have you learned about your partner? What have you learned about yourself?

Variations

None

JERK

Subsidiary Goal(s)

a. To explore the dynamics involved in creative movement.

b. To gain insight into the process of fantasy.

c. To examine members' perceptions.

Group Application

Twelve members or less. To be used with encounter, personal growth, marathon and t-groups. Best results are obtained if the exercise is used with members who have had prior exposure to sensory awareness.

Application Variables

Fifteen minutes. The exercise is 100 per cent non-verbal. The room must be large enough to allow members unrestricted movement.

Administrative Procedure

a. The facilitator makes the following statement: "In learning how to move we often find it very difficult to "let go" of our control over our body. Being able to truly move is more than simply moving various limbs. It means you are able to flow. This exercise is designed to let us over-control ourselves. This helps us exaggerate our movements and block out true flowing motions. Please spread out within the room so that you may move about comfortably without feeling unduly restrained."

b. After all members have spread out within the room, the facilitator states: "I would like you to begin by moving your arms in a very jerky manner. Pretend you are a robot. Move your legs in the same manner. You may either move about the room or remain standing in the same space."

c. Once members have gotten the movement down pat, the facilitator states: "Using the same jerky motion, I want you to begin to imitate yourself. Feel free to move any part(s) of your body. Go as fast or as slow as you wish. Become aware of your movements. Try and make sure you are always in control—don't let go!"

d. After several minutes, he continues: "Begin to let go of the control you have over your motions. Begin to let them flow *without* control. Your movements no longer need to be jerky. Let yourself go free—float—move—flow."

e. When the facilitator feels all members have reached a degree of letting go of their motions, the members rejoin the large group for processing.

Suggestions for Facilitator Process

Concentrate on the following during processing:

a. How did you feel during the initial stages of the exercise? Did your feelings change as time went on? If so, in what way?

b. Did you move about the room or stay in the same spot? Why? What were you aware of while you were moving? How did you imitate yourself?

c. What roles did fantasy and creativity play in your movements? Did you reach a point where you felt you were able to let go? How did the "letting go" feelings compare with those feelings you had when you were over-controlling yourself?

Variations

None

*LEG LIFT

Subsidiary Goal(s)

a. To gain insight into bodily flows of energy.

b. To increase awareness of the dynamics involved in dependency.

c. To gain greater insight into the relationship between muscles.

Group Application

Twelve members or less. Since dyads are used, group size should be even . To be used with encounter, personal growth, marathon and t-groups.

Application Variables

Forty-five minutes to one hour. The exercise is 100 per cent non-verbal. The room should be large enough to allow the dyads to spread out unrestrained. The ideal setting has a carpeted floor and means of darkening the room (e.g. shades, light dampers, etc.) . Candles may be used to enhance the effect.

Administrative Procedure

a. The members are told to non-verbally mill around and form dyads.

b. The facilitator then tells the dyads: "Find a spot in the room where you feel comfortable and which affords you some privacy."

c. When all dyads are situated, he continues: "Please remove your shoes and socks. Then, one of the dyadic partners is to lie on the floor, on his back, with his eyes closed."

d. When this is accomplished, the facilitator says: "Those of you who are standing are to take hold of your partner's foot. Which foot does not matter.
   Place one hand beneath the heel and the other around the ankle."

e. The facilitator tells the supine member: "Let your leg muscles go completely limp. Relax! Let it be so limp and relaxed that only your partner's hold on it stops it from falling."

f. After a minute, he says to the standing member: "Very gently and very slowly lift the foot from the floor. If your partner has not let his leg go limp, it will feel quite tight. If this is the case, gently place it back on the floor. Wait a few minutes and try again."

g. He continues: "As you lift the foot, you will come to a point where the knee should be bent toward the chest of your partner. As the leg bends, keep lifting. When you sense strain, stop. Start then to return the foot to its original position." (The entire lift should last approximately five minutes. It should not be hurried.) .

h. The facilitator tells the supine members: "When your foot is again on the floor, take a few minutes to silently explore your feelings and the sensations of your foot and leg.
   When you are ready, signal to your partner that you are ready to have your other leg lifted."

i. Steps *e* through *g* are repeated.

j. After this, both legs are to be lifted simultaneously. The facilitator says to the members lying down: "Try to be aware of any similarities and differences in the feelings and sensations of your legs."

k. When the member lying down is ready, the positions are reversed and the entire sequence is repeated.

Suggestions for Facilitator Process

Concentrate on the following during processing:

a. Was it difficult for you to let your leg relax and go limp? Why? What feelings did you have? What sensations did your leg have? What was going on in the rest of your body?

b. How did you feel about holding your partner's foot? What feelings did you have as you lifted the leg? What were you aware of in yourself? In your partner? Which was most enjoyable, lifting or being lifted? Why?

Variations

None

*LISTEN!

Subsidiary Goal(s)

a. To learn that increasing one's listening skills can lead to increasing other sensory skills.

b. To learn that "hearing" equals "labeling" and that "listening" equals "awareness" and "feeling."

Group Application

Group size is unlimited. However, if processing is to occur, the group size should be twenty or less. Applicable to any group. Especially helpful when used with classroom and t-groups whenever the facilitator wants the members to investigate the differences between hearing and listening.

Application Variables

Ten to fifteen minutes. The exercise is 100 per cent non-verbal. Access to the outdoors is desirable and will help accentuate the learning involved.

Administrative Procedure

a. The facilitator says: "We will take the opportunity today to improve our listening skills. Let's go outside." If access to the outdoors is impossible, the facilitator should open all doors and windows. This helps increase the available sound stimuli.

b. When all are seated he says: "Close your eyes and cup your hands over your ears. Then uncup them. Do this five times and listen to the sound."

c. When all are finished, he says: "I want you to put your fingers in your ears. Try to shut off *all* sound. You will still *hear*. Listen to what you hear."

d. After a minute, he says: "Now, close your eyes and listen. Dive into and identify the sounds."

e. After three minutes, he continues: "During the last phase of this exercise you heard sounds very accurately and accutely. But, I doubt that you really listened to them.

You heard the train, the breathing, the wind, and so on. But, did you listen? Try now to *listen* to the sound. Ignore the source. Don't label it, just listen to it.

As you do this, listen rather than hear, note how the labels are so inadequate as representations of the sounds."

f. After five minutes, he says: "Let's discuss this experience."

Suggestions for Facilitator Process

Concentrate on the following during processing:

a. What have you learned about the difference between hearing and listening? How did you learn this? Why did you learn it?

b. Was I right that you *heard* labels? If so, why? Were you able to ignore the labels and *listen* to the sounds? If so, yes and why? If no, why not?

c. Were you aware of an increase in listening skills? How and why? When were you more "aware," when you were "hearing" or listening"? Why?

Variations

None

ME—YOU

Subsidiary Goal(s)

a. To give and receive feedback.
b. To gain greater insight into members' perceptions.
c. To facilitate creativity.

Group Application

Twelve members or less. To be used with any group concerned with creative feedback and awareness.

Application Variables

Thirty minutes. The exercise is 70 per cent non-verbal and 30 per cent verbal. Paper and crayons are required for each member.

Administrative Procedure

a. The facilitator passes out paper and crayons to the members and asks that they find a semi-private space within the room.
b. The following instructions are then given: "I would like you to close your eyes and become aware of what you are, what you feel, and what you think. As you are becoming aware of yourself, I want you to let your hand draw on the paper whatever you are feeling. Remember to *keep your eyes closed*. Let your drawing be. Let it flow. Try not to control it or give it direction. You will be given ten minutes. Please begin."
c. After ten minutes the facilitator says: "Open your eyes. Look at your drawing. Now look around the room. Silently begin to draw a picture of one of the members in the group. Draw him with regard to who he is, not what he looks like."
d. After ten minutes, the group reforms and the drawings are displayed. Members are encouraged to discuss their second drawing with the member the individual had in mind when he drew it.
e. After sharing and displaying pictures, the members discuss the experience.

Suggestions for Facilitator Process

Concentrate on the following during processing:

a. What were you aware of when you began to draw the first picture? Did the images flow or were they forced? Were you surprised when you opened your eyes and saw what you had drawn? Why?

b. How did you draw your second picture? What were you aware of during this time? If you were drawn by another member, were you surprised at the results? Why?

Variations

None

MANIPULATION

Subsidiary Goal(s)

a. To examine members' perceptions.
b. To gain greater insight into the process of communication.
c. To cope with tension

Group Application

Twelve members or less. To be used with encounter, personal growth, marathon and t-groups.

Application Variables

Thirty minutes. The exercise is 100 per cent non-verbal. The room must be large enough to allow members to move about unrestrained.

Administrative Procedure

a. The facilitator asks members to spread out within the room and assume a comfortable position. The following instructions are then given: "Close your eyes and think of some behavior which you exhibit intentionally to manipulate other people. If possible think of a behavior which you have exhibited within the group. Bring your attention to the way you manipulate and to what end it serves."

b. After several minutes the facilitator states: "Try and *become* the behavior you have in mind. For example if you manipulate by crying, become the tears. Let yourself feel your behavior. Become aware of what your body is now saying to you. Listen to the messages your body is sending to you."

c. After several more minutes the facilitator adds: "Try and see the person or people you are manipulating. Notice their reactions, their feelings and their expressions. Become aware of the interaction between both or all of you. Let the images and scenes unfold before your eyes."

d. When the facilitator feels enough time has elapsed to allow members to fully experience their awareness, the following is stated: "Reverse roles. Become aware of the times you have been manipulated. Get in touch with how you felt. If possible relate this experience to the group. Listen to your body as you experience this. Again try to let the images and scenes flow. When you feel you have fully absorbed the experience, slowly disassociate yourself from it, then open your eyes and rejoin the group."

Suggestions for Facilitator Process

Concentrate on the following during processing:

a. How did you view yourself manipulating people? How did it make you feel? What messages did your body give you? Did you become aware of any new insights? What are they?

b. What did you learn when you saw yourself being the manipulator? Did your experiences relate to the group? If so, how? How did you feel when you became the behavior that was intended to manipulate?

c. What feelings did you have when the roles were reversed? What differences did you become aware of in terms of your body between being manipulator and being manipulated? Do you feel you have been manipulated within the group? If so, how? How have you manipulated the group or its members?

Variations

None

MECHANICS

Subsidiary Goal(s)

a. To increase awareness of body movement and functions.

b. To gain insight into the dynamics involved in non-verbal communication.

c. To emphasize various levels of communication.

Group Application

Twelve members or less. To be used with encounter, personal growth, marathon and t-groups. Best results are obtained if the exercise is utilized after the group has had ample sessions to allow for the lessening of inhibitions.

Application Variables

Thirty minutes. The exercise is 100 per cent non-verbal. The room should be large enough to allow members to move about unrestrained.

Administrative Procedure

a. The facilitator asks members to stand up and to loosen their bodies.

b. He then makes the following statement: "I would like you all to become mechanical beings—machines which move very deliberately and very stiffly. There are to be no words. You can make sounds which may represent clanking, squeaking, whirling, etc."

c. The facilitator then asks all members to begin. He urges them to try to discover the types of machine the other members are. He urges them to interact with the other machines in the room.

d. Physical contact should be encouraged as well as movement between members.

e. After 20 minutes the facilitator is to instruct each member to begin the process of wearing or winding down.

f. After 10 minutes the group discusses the experience.

Suggestions for Facilitator Process

Concentrate on the following during processing:

a. What type of machine did you discover you were? What type of sounds were you making, and what did they represent? Did you feel you were actually communicating with the other members? If so, what was said?

b. How much physical contact was there between yourself and other members? How did you feel when you were instructed to wear down? What have you learned about your own body? What did you learn about other members' bodies?

Variations

None

*NON-VERBAL MEAL—DYADIC

Subsidiary Goal(s)

a. To gain insight into interdependency.

b. To explore the dynamics involved in the development of cooperative behavior.

c. To become more in touch with non-verbal cues.

d. To establish greater and more meaningful relationships.

e. To achieve a peak experience.

Group Application

Twelve members or less. To be used with any group wishing to explore cooperation and interdependence in an intimate environment. It is suggested that the exercise be used only with groups that have had considerable exposure to sensory awareness experiences and whose members have established considerable warmth and care for one another.

Application Variables

One hour. The exercise is 100 per cent non-verbal. Towels, access to washing facilities or a basin of warm water for each dyad, and food are required (no eating utensils except plates are used).

The following menu is suggested for its symbolic and sensory value: fried chicken, cold cuts, potato salad, potato chips, sliced tomatoes, sliced cheese, sliced carrots, sliced bananas, raisins, nuts, unsliced loaves of bread, butter, various fruits (unpeeled and unsliced), beverages, napkins, paper plates, cups, and tooth picks.

Food should be prepared and laid out in advance, but kept from view. Sufficient space is necessary for the dyads to be relatively isolated from one another. Access to the outdoors is also desirable.

Administrative Procedure

a. The facilitator should inform all members in advance that they should be prepared to: eat a meal, bring a towel and wear comfortable clothing. The cost of the meal will be approximately $1.00 per member, depending on the size of the total group. The facilitator may wish to ask each member to pay for his share of the meal.
b. The facilitator asks members to non-verbally form dyads with members they feel particularly close to.
c. Each dyad begins their meal after being given the following specific instructions:

1. No verbal communication throughout the entire meal.
2. All activities are to take place in dyad.
3. No utensils may be used.
4. Dyads begin by washing one another's hands.
5. No member may select his own plate.
6. At the conclusion, the members may wish to pick each other's teeth, wash each other's hands, give back or body massages, etc.

Suggestions for Facilitator Process

Concentrate on the following during processing:

a. What have you learned about your partner? About yourself? How did you decide which member would be fed first? What did you learn about dependency?
b. What type of non-verbal cues did you give your partner? Did

you receive from your partner? Which foods had special meaning for you?

c. Did you enjoy more feeding or being fed? Why? What type of messages was your body sending to you during the experience? Have your feelings toward your partner changed in any way? If so, in what way?

Variations

None

NON-VERBAL MEAL—GROUP[2]

Subsidiary Goal(s)

a. To explore the dynamics involved in the development of cooperative behavior.
b. To gain insight into interdependency.
c. To provide an atmosphere for group relaxation and fun.

Group Application

Twelve members or less. To be used with any group wishing to explore cooperation and interdependence in an intimate environment.

Application Variables

One hour. The exercise is 100 per cent non-verbal. Towels, access to washing facilities or a basin of warm water for each subgroup, and food are required (no eating utensils except plates are used.)

The following menu is suggested for its symbolic and sensory value: Fried chicken, potato salad, potato chips, sliced tomatoes, sliced cheese, sliced carrots, sliced bananas, raisins, nuts, unsliced loaves of bread, butter, various fruits (unpeeled and unsliced), beverages, napkins, paper plates, cups, and tooth picks.

---

[2]This is an adaptation of an exercise developed by Robert Brook and Robert Shelton, University of Kansas.

Food should be prepared and laid out in advance, but kept from view. Sufficient space is necesasry for subgroups to be relatively isolated from one another.

Administrative Procedure

a. The facilitator should inform all participants in advance that they should be prepared to: Eat a meal, bring a towel, and wear comfortable clothing. The cost of the meal will be approximately $1.00 per member, depending on the size of the total group. The facilitator may wish to ask each member to pay for his share of the meal.

b. The total group is divided into 5 or 6 subgroups. Odd or even numbers will make a difference in feeding interaction. The selection process chosen should be appropriate to the level of the group's development (random, self selection, assignment by facilitator, etc.) .

c. Participants begin their meal after being given the following specific instructions:

    1. No verbal communication throughout the meal experience, beginning now.

    2. All activities are to be done in the subgroups.

    3. Each member is to attend to other subgroup member's needs, but is not to attend to his own needs. (example —washing and feeding others, but not one's self) . The only exception is the selection of one's own plate of food.

    4. *No* utensils.

    5. Subgroups begin by washing and drying each others' hands.

    6. Group members go to the buffet table together. Each member selects his own food and the subgroup finds a place to eat.

    7. Members feed each other within the subgroups.

    8. At the conclusion, the members may wish to pick each others' teeth, wash each others' hands, give back or body massages, etc.

Suggestions for Facilitator Process

Concentrate on the following during processing:

a. What type of cooperation did you receive? What type did you give? How did you feel about being dependent upon other members for food? How intimate did you feel towards the other members?

b. How did you view the total experience? Did you experience satisfaction and/or fun? Was there any time you felt frustrated? If so, when?

Variations

None

*OBJECTS #2

Subsidiary Goal(s)

a. To explore member perceptions.
b. To gain new insights into inanimate objects.
c. To learn the part visual projection plays in stereotyping.

Group Application

Twelve members or less. To be used with any group concerned with sensory awareness, but most frequently used with encounter, personal growth, marathon and t-groups.

Application Variables

Thirty minutes. The exercise is 100 per cent non-verbal. One blindfold is needed for each member. A variety of inanimate objects, e.g. pencils, balls, flowers, paper, yarn, etc., are required.

Administrative Procedure

a. The facilitator gives a blindfold to each member and then says: "I would like each member to put on a blindfold and become as silent as possible. I will hand each of you an object. When you receive it I want you to explore your object by touching, tasting, smelling and listening to it. When

I say pass, I want you to hand your object over to the member to the right of you and receive a new object from the member on your left." The facilitator should have members pass their object approximately every 60 seconds.

b. After all members have had an opportunity to explore each object, the facilitator states: "Lie back and absorb the experience. Let your body rest while you think about the sensations you have experienced. After you feel you have reached a point of relaxation I want you to explore your own body in the same manner in which you explored the objects."

c. After several minutes, he continues: "When you feel ready, remove your blindfold and sit up. We will then discuss this experience."

Suggestions for Facilitator Process

Concentrate on the following during processing:

a. Did you immediately recognize your objects? Did you discover any new sensations? How did one object differ from the other?

b. Was your awareness increased by not being able to visually observe the object? How did you feel as you explored your own body? Did you discover any surprises?

Variations

None

OBJECTS #3

Subsidiary Goal(s)

a. To explore the process of fantasy.
b. To facilitate creativity.
c. To explore members' perceptions

Group Application

Twelve members or less. To be used with encounter, personal growth, marathon and t-groups. Best results are obtained if the exercise is used in the latter stage of group development.

Application Variables

Twenty to thirty minutes. The exercise is 100 per cent non-verbal. A number of miscellaneous objects are needed. For example, book, paper, balloon, ball, chair, light bulb, food, etc. The room must be large enough to allow members unrestricted movement.

Administrative Procedure

a. The facilitator gives the following introduction: "Most of us are not very aware of the objects which surround us every day. When we sit in a chair, how often do we notice its shape, texture, smell, feel, etc.? A great awareness of inanimate objects can greatly enhance one's appreciation of beauty. I have brought a number of common objects with me. I am going to ask you to pick one of these objects and study it for a few minutes."

b. After several minutes, the facilitator continues: "I would now like a volunteer to come into the center of the circle with his object."

c. After the volunteer has taken his place, the facilitator tells him: "Become your object. Use any method you feel appropriate, as long as it is done non-verbally. Try and actually *become* your object. Don't just imitate it. Your presentation may be as long or as short as you wish." The facilitator may wish to give an example. For instance, a member who has selected a marble may wish to "roll" among the group members. Or, he may simply assume the shape of the marble, emphasizing its transparency.

d. After each member has been given an opportunity to become his object, the members discuss the experience.

Suggestions for Facilitator Process

Concentrate on the following during processing:

a. What did you first notice about the object you chose? Why did you choose that object? Do you now perceive it differerently than you normally do?

b. What type of process did you go through in becoming your

object? Do you feel you actually became your object? What role did fantasy and creativity play for you during the exercise?

c. Have you gained any new insights? What are they? Were you surprised at any of the other members' presentations? If so, which ones and why?

Variations

None

*ODORS

Subsidiary Goal(s)

a. To explore members' perceptions.

b. To create an environment conducive to "playful" learning.

Group Application

Twelve members or less. Since dyads are used, group size should be even. To be used with encounter, personal growth, marathon and t-groups. Best results are obtained if the exercise is used with members who have had considerable exposure to sensory awareness.

Application Variables

Thirty to forty-five minutes. The exercise is 100 per cent non-verbal. The following items are needed: a napkin soaked in perfume, a flower, leather objects, tabasco sauce, cinnamon, onions, leaves, pepper, a jar full of dirt, a piece of bread, a book, a wet towel and a glass full of a carbonated beverage. Other items having distinct odors may be substituted at the facilitator's discretion.

Administrative Procedure

a. The facilitator asks the members to non-verbally form dyads.

b. The following instructions are then given: "Decide which one of you will be the first to experience a sensory experience. When you have decided, find a semi-private spot within the room. The member experiencing the exercise is to be seated comfortably with his eyes closed. The other member is to select an object from the pile and bring it back to his partner."

c. After the selections have been made, the facilitator continues: "I want you to hold the object you have selected in front of your partner's nose. Do not let him touch it. I want the members smelling the object to become aware of its fragrance. Get in touch with your own reaction to the odor. Listen to the messages your body is sending to you. Please begin."

d. After several minutes, the members are told to return their object to the original pile and select another object. Step *c* is then repeated. Each member should have the opportunity to smell five or more objects.

e. After members have had exposure to several objects, roles are reversed and steps *b* through *d* are repeated.

Suggestions for Facilitator Process

Concentrate on the following during processing:

a. *To members smelling the object:* Did you know what the object was by its odor? What odors struck you as the most pleasant? Why? The most offensive? Why?

b. How well did you get to know your object through smell? What messages did your body send to you? Were you aware of your partner holding the object?

c. *To members holding the object:* How did you select the objects to be explored by your partner? What type of non-verbal cues did your partner send during the experience? What else were you aware of during the experience?

Variations

None

PARTS

Subsidiary Goal(s)

a. To give and receive feedback.
b. To gain self-insight.
c. To explore the dynamics involved in movement.

Group Application

Twelve members or less. Since dyads are used, group size should be even. To be used with encounter, personal growth, marathon and t-groups.

Application Variables

Ten to fifteen minutes. The exercise is 80 per cent non-verbal and 20 per cent verbal. The room must be large enough to allow the dyads to spread out without feeling unduly restricted.

Administrative Procedure

a. The facilitator asks the members to non-verbally form dyads and spread out within the room.

b. After all members have paired off, the facilitator gives the following instructions: "Whenever we make a movement or gesture, there are usually many body structures involved. For example, when we shake hands not only our hands are moving, but also our forearms, arms, chest, head and neck. Because our awareness is focused on one part of our body we tend to lose most of the information the rest of our body is sending to us.
Stand up with your partner and reach out and touch each others' arms. I want you to do this several times. Become aware of each part of your body that moves."

c. After two to three minutes, he says: "Now repeat the same gesture in slow motion. This time concentrate on your partner's body. Become aware of what is moving. Notice your partner's breathing."

d. After several minutes, the facilitator states: "Sit down with your partner and begin to discuss the experience. Give one another feedback on how you were being perceived. As you are doing this become aware of what parts of your body are moving as a result of speaking."

e. After several more minutes, the group rejoins for processing.

Suggestions for Facilitator Process

Concentrate on the following during processing:

a. What parts of your body moved as you touched your partner? Were there any surprises? If so, what? What parts of your partner's body did you become aware of when you were being touched?

b. What insights did you gain? What feedback did you receive from your partner when you sat down and talked? Do you feel it was accurate?

c. What parts of your body moved as you spoke? What messages was your body sending to you?

Variations

None

PLAYING WITH BALLOONS

Subsidiary Goal(s)

a. To encourage participation.

b. To develop insight into one's feelings about giving and receiving.

Group Application

Twenty members or less. Most effective when used with groups of twelve or less. Applicable to any group, but most frequently used with encounter, personal growth, marathon and t-groups.

Application Variables

Fifteen to thirty minutes. The exercise is 80 per cent non-verbal and 20 per cent verbal. The room must be large enough to allow members to be able to separate sufficiently enough to have a feeling of private space. A large *assortment* of balloons is needed. The assortment should be large enough that there are three to five choices of balloons per member.

Administrative Procedure

a. The facilitator places the assortment of balloons on the floor. He then says: "Non-verbally, go to the pile and take a balloon. Feel free to take more than one."

b. When all members have made their selection(s), the facilitator says: "Blow up your balloon as much or as little as you wish. If you took more than one balloon, feel free to blow up more than one. When you are satisfied, tie a knot in the end."

c. When all members have finished, the facilitator says: "Now, mill around. Show your balloon to others. Let them explore it. If you wish to give and/or receive balloons, do so."

d. When it becomes apparent that the milling is finished, the facilitator says: "Now, go to each other and tell why you chose the balloon you did, how you feel about playing with balloons, why your balloon is inflated to the extent it is."

e. When the members have finished, the facilitator says: "Find a spot in the room where you feel you have some privacy. Then sit down."

f. After all are seated, he continues: "Rub the balloons on your cheeks, face, head, neck and body. Be aware of your feelings, of the images that emerge in your mind. Concentrate on the texture of the balloon and of the movements it has."

g. After three to five minutes, the facilitator says: "Now, make noises with your balloon. Pay attention to the various noises and sounds. Try to determine what these noises remind you of and what images they bring to mind."

h. After three to five minutes, the facilitator says: "Now break your balloon. Do it any way you wish to. Be aware of your feelings as you do this."

Suggestions for Facilitator Process

Concentrate on the following during processing:

a. Why did you take the balloon(s) you did? Why did you inflate the balloons as you did? Did you give away any balloons? If not, why not? If yes, why? How did you feel when you gave or received a balloon?

b. What images and feelings did you have as you explored your balloon? What senses were you aware of? What feelings and images did you have as you made noises with the balloons?

c. How did you break your balloon? Why did you break it in the manner you chose? How did you feel during and after the breaking?

Variations

None

ROCK EMPATHY[3]

Subsidiary Goal(s)

a. To learn that everything, even inanimate objects, is unique.
b. To develop insight into one's feelings about giving and receiving.
c. To develop insight into one's feelings about closeness and separation.

Group Application

Group size is unlimited, although most exercises will be used with groups of twelve or less, Applicable to any group.

Application Variables

Forty minutes for a group of twelve or less. The exercise is 100 per cent non-verbal. The facilitator should provide a large assortment of rocks and stones of different sizes, colors and textures. He should bring four or five more than is required to insure that some selection is provided.

Administrative Procedure

a. The facilitator dumps the rock assortment on the floor and says: "Come and pick out a rock. Try to pick one you have some "feel" for. Then, go back to your place."
b. The facilitator removes the extra rocks and says: "Close your eyes. Examine your rocks using your sense of touch. Try to discover its shape, texture, hardness, idiosyncrosies, and so on. Try to become the rock."
c. After five minutes, the facilitator explains that it will be helpful if each member can feel that the rock is a "part" of his self. He asks that the rocks be placed on the body. Two minutes per sequence is recommended. He should ask that

[3]Adapted from an exercise developed by Judy Morris, Counselor, West Intermediate School, Mt. Pleasant, Michigan.

the members "try to become aware of the different body reactions and feelings you have at each stage."

    1. "Lying down, with your back on the floor, place the
rock on your forehead."

    2. "Lie on your stomach and place the rock at the back
of your neck."

    3. "Lie on your back and place the rock on your chest."

    4. "Place it on your stomach."

    5. "Place it on your knees."

    6. "Stand and place it under your feet."

    7. "Hold the rock above your head. Feel and be aware of
its weight."

d. After step 7, the facilitator says: "Get in touch with how
close you are to your rock. Hold it in your right hand and
tenderly show it how you feel toward it."

e. After a few minutes, he continues: "Now, slowly move the
rock to your left hand. Notice the differences in feeling due
to using your left hand."

f. After a few minutes, the facilitator says: "Slowly move the
rock from left hand to right, right to left, and so on. Be
aware of the rock's feelings for being moved about. Be the
rock."

g. After a minute or two, he continues: "We will now share
our rocks. Pass your rock to the person on your left.

Discover, feel, be the new rock. Note how it is similar to
and different from your previous rock. Then, pass the rock
to the left. Continue passing and exploring until you receive your original rock."

h. When step *g* has been completed, the facilitator says: "Take
some time to rediscover your rock. Remember the other
rocks and try to compare and contrast your rock with them."

i. After two minutes, the facilitator says: "We will now part
with our rocks by giving them to other members. Find someone, go to him and give him your rock. Try to make the
giving personal."

Suggestions for Facilitator Process

Concentrate on the following during processing:

a. Why did you select the rock you did? Did your feelings for it change as the exercise progressed? How? Why? How did you feel when you got your original rock back?

b. How did you feel about giving your rock to another member? What criteria did you use for giving your rock away? Was it easier to give a rock away or receive one? Why?

c. Did anyone not receive a rock? How do you feel about this? Who received more than one rock? Why? How did you feel about receiving more than one?

Variations

None

*ROCKS

Subsidiary Goal(s)

a. To gain greater awareness of inanimate objects.

b. To learn that everyone is truly unique.

c. To become aware of the differences in one's sensory development.

d. To learn that one usually uses one sense in forming evaluations, judgements and impressions.

Group Application

Twelve members or less. To be used with encounter, personal growth, marathon and t-groups. Most effective if used in the latter stages of the group's life.

Application Variables

Fifty to sixty minutes. The exercise is 60 per cent non-verbal and 40 per cent verbal. A spacious outdoor environment is most ideal. However, if access to the outdoors is not available, the facilitator should bring a large assortment of rocks. There should be a sufficent number of rocks that each member has three to five choices. (See Administrative Procedure, step *a*.)

Administrative Procedure

a. If the group is outdoors, the facilitator says: "Spread out and explore. Do this alone and non-verbally. You are to search for and bring back a rock. Have a reason for choosing your rock. You have five minutes."

If the group is inside, the facilitator dumps his assortment on the floor and says: "Come and get a rock. Have a reason for choosing it. Then go back to your place and sit quietly."

b. When all members have taken (or found) a rock and are seated, the facilitator says: "You have thirty minutes to get to know your rock. Become aware of its shape, color, texture, feel, weight, etc. Learn its "personality." Do your best to be the rock."

c. After thirty minutes, the facilitator says: "I would now like you to verbally share your rock with us. Give it a name and introduce it to us. Tell us about it. Share its "personality" with us."

d. After each member has presented his rock to the group, the members discuss the experience.

Suggestions for Facilitator Process

Concentrate on the following during processing:

a. What were your reasons for selecting your rock? Did you feel "silly" at any time? Why? How did you cope with this feeling?

b. What did you learn about inanimate objects? How does this learning apply to people? What did you learn about yourself?

c. Why did you give your rock its name? How close was its personality to yours? What was your rock's best feature? What was its worse feature? Do you want to keep it? Why? Why not?

Variations

Variation I

a. Any inanimate object may be substituted for rocks. For example, one could use nuts, bolts, nails, pencils, etc.

b. The same Administrative Procedure as listed in the original exercise is then followed.

*SENSORY COLLAGE

Subsidiary Goal(s)

a. To experience a variety of intense sensations.
b. To experience the process of fantasy.
c. To become more in touch with thoughts and feelings.
d. To gain greater self-insight.
e. To explore perceptions.
f. To explore feelings concerning physical contact.

Group Application

Twelve members or less. To be used with encounter, personal growth, marathon and t-groups.

Application Variables

One and a half to two hours. The exercise is 60 per cent non-verbal and 40 per cent verbal. The room must be large enough to allow members unrestrained movement. A darkened room, lighted only by candles, is recommended.

Administrative Procedure

a. The facilitator asks members to remove shoes and socks and assume a comfortable position. He then makes the following statement: "We are about to search the depth of our awareness. For the next two hours we will engage in a variety of experiences intended to increase our capacity of awareness. I would like to begin by asking that you close your eyes and silently ask yourself what you are aware of right at this moment. Your awareness may be of your own body, sounds, feelings, etc. Try and focus your energy upon whatever you are aware of. Try to reach an even greater level and depth of awareness."

b. After several minutes, he says: "If you find your awareness shifting from one sensation to the other, don't worry. Keep on letting it flow. Let the sensations fade in and out as they come to you. Try not to direct your attention. Instead try to be attentive."

c. After several more minutes, he continues: "Try and become aware of as much as possible. Instead of focusing in on one sensation try and let yourself be bombarded by sensations."

d. When the facilitator feels the group has achieved a point of "letting go," the following instructions are given: "Lie back with your eyes still closed and slowly, starting at the top of your head, force the awareness and sensation downward. Let it flow and move toward your neck, down your arms, through your chest, through your stomach, down your legs and on out through your toes. You are now a vacuum, void of sensation—simply floating. Please rest."

e. After five minutes, the facilitator says: "Open your mouth as wide as possible and slowly begin to take deep breaths. As you breathe get in touch with the air you are letting into your body. Notice where it goes after it travels into your lungs and through your chest. Become aware of your body and how it is reacting to your full and deep breathing."

f. After several minutes, he says: "Become aware of the sensations outside your body. For the next several minutes I want you to focus your attention back and forth from inside your body to outside your body. Try and get in touch with the interactions between your physical being and the physical world. Go back and forth several times, each time trying to integrate yourself, your awareness and your perceptions of the physical world."

g. After ten minutes, the facilitator gives the following instructions: "I would like you to gradually increase your awareness of the physical world. When you feel ready, sit up and open your eyes. Take several minutes to look around you and at yourself."

h. After all members have opened their eyes and are sitting up, the facilitator says: "I would like you all to stand. Walk around. As you walk, look at the other members' eyes. When you feel comfortable with another member I would like you to non-verbally pair off and find a spot in the room where you both may be seated comfortably."

i. After all members have paired off into dyads, the following instructions are given: "Please be seated, facing one another. Close your eyes and touch hands with your partner. Get in touch with the other member's hands. Pay close attention to texture of the skin, warmth, shape, weight, etc." After several minutes, the facilitator adds: "Let your partner know what you are now aware of by use of your hands only."

j. When the facilitator feels that all members have had ample time to non-verbally express their awareness, the following is added: "Touch your partner's face. Feel the person as well as the skin. Now become aware of your own body. What is it saying to you? Let your partner know what you are feeling by continuing to touch each other's face."

k. After ten to fifteen minutes, the facilitator says: "Slowly open your eyes and discuss the following with your partner. What were you aware of while touching? I want you to begin each sentence with, I was aware of. . . . After you both feel that you have honestly discussed what you were aware of, I would like you to discuss anything that you were afraid to be aware of during contact with your partner. After discussing that I would like you to speak about what you are aware of right now." Twenty to thirty minutes should be allowed for this dyadic discussion.

l. When all members feel that they have meaningfully discussed their awarenesses and feelings with their partner, the facilitator asks them to come together in a large circle and assume a comfortable position.

m. The facilitator then asks members to slowly try to re-achieve a degree of relaxation and awareness both within and without themselves. After several minutes, processing begins.

Suggestions for Facilitator Process

Concentrate on the following during processing:

a. What types of sensations were you originally aware of? Did you find that your awareness shifted often? If so, in what

way? How much "control" did you have over your awareness?

b. Were you able to let the sensations flow? If not, why not?
What did you experience when I asked you to force your
awareness through and out your body? What types of awareness did you have about your body? To what extent were
you aware of your fantasies and images? How were these
symbolic of you as a person?

c. What type of process took place when I asked you to open
your eyes? How did you select your partner? What did you
experience with your partner? How do you now feel toward
him? Why do you think your feelings for your partner
changed?

d. Did you avoid or leave out any awareness intentionally?
What were you aware of in the here and now? How did that
differ from talking about the awareness you had experienced
a short time before?

Variations

None

*SENSORY DEPRIVATION

Subsidiary Goal(s)

a. To explore the dynamics involved in isolation.
b. To experience aloneness.
c. To discover inner resources.

Group Application

Twelve members or less. To be used with encounter, personal
growth, marathon and t-groups. The exercise should only be
used with groups whose members have had extensive exposure
to sensory awareness.

Application Variables

One hour and thirty minutes. The exercise is 100 per cent non-
verbal. The following list of items is required: one blindfold for
each member, a large amount of cotton, four pillows for each

member and a nose clip for each person. The room should be large enough to allow members to spread out without feeling unduly restricted. Insulation from outside noise is also desired.

Administrative Procedure

a. The facilitator gives the following introduction: "We all depend on our senses in order to communicate with the world. I suspect very few of us, if any, have ever simulated or experienced sensory deprivation. This simply means cutting our imput and feedback of sensory stimuli to a minimum. For the next hour and thirty minutes we are going to try and cut out as much sensory stimulation as possible. First of all, I want you to spread out within the room and find a spot where you can lie down without touching any objects."

b. After all members have spread out, the facilitator passes out the blindfolds, pillows and cotton. He then says: "Before we start the experience, if at any time during the exercise you feel that you are just too uncomfortable, please feel free to get up and stop. If this occurs please be as silent as possible.

I would like everyone to put on the blindfolds. Once this is completed, place one pillow under your head, one under each arm and one under your feet. During the exercise there is to be a minimal amount of movement on your part."

e. After all members have been blindfolded and have positioned the pillows according to directions, the facilitator tells them to place the cotton in their ears and the nose plug in their noses. Before this is done, the facilitator says: "I will turn out the lights as soon as everyone has placed the cotton in their ears. I will turn on the lights in one hour and thirty minutes. During this time there will be no other directions." (The facilitator may wish to set an alarm clock next to him in order to keep track of the time.)

Suggestions for Facilitator Process

Concentrate on the following during processing:

a. What did you experience during the past hour and thirty minutes? Which of your senses did you feel the most loss for?

Which did you lose first? Did you feel panicky? How did you cope with it?

b. What were you aware of during the experience? Did your mood change as time went on? What insights did you gain about yourself?

Variations

None

SILENT DIALOGUE

Subsidiary Goal(s)

a. To gain greater insight into self-awareness.
b. To explore and deal with inner conflicts.

Group Application

Twelve members or less. To be used with encounter, personal growth, marathon and t-groups. Best results are obtained if the exercise is used after ample sessions have elapsed to have allowed for self-exploration.

Application Variables

Fifteen minutes. The exercise is 100 per cent non-verbal.

Administrative Procedure

a. The facilitator asks each member to sit comfortably and close his eyes.
b. He then says: "Form a visual image of yourself as if you were seated in front of a large mirror. Pay special attention to the image which you have created (i.e., facial expression, body position, dress, etc.) ."
c. Each member is now told: "Silently criticize the image seated in front of you. Try to be as critical as you can. Remember your criticisms."
d. The member is then told: "Silently answer or respond to the criticisms that you confronted your "mirror image" with."
e. After several minutes, the members discuss the experience.

Suggestions for Facilitator Process

Concentrate on the following during processing:

a. Was it difficult for you to create an image of yourself? Why? Were you surprised at what you created? What type of criticisms did you formulate?

b. How did you respond to your criticisms? What have you learned about yourself?

Variations

None

SPACE EFFECTS

Subsidiary Goal(s)

a. To learn that concepts of space are continually changing.

b. To learn the conditions and variables which affect one's concepts of space.

Group Application

Twenty members or less. Applicable to any group, but most frequently used with encounter, personal growth, marathon and t-groups.

Application Variables

Ten to fifteen minutes. The exercise is 100 per cent non-verbal. The room must be large enough to allow the members to space themselves sufficiently enough to develop a feeling of private space.

Administrative Procedure

a. The facilitator says: "So that we may learn that space is not static, that it is always changing with regard to its effect on us, spread out around the room so there is sufficient distance between each of you that you feel some degree of privacy."

b. When all members are situated, he says: "Turn and face the wall. Stand about fifteen feet from it. Stand quietly and observe the location and distance and space."

c. After a minute the facilitator continues: "Now walk the distance. Be aware of any changes in your perception of the space, distance and location. When you reach the wall, touch it and explore it. When you have finished this, turn around and walk back to where you were originally standing."

d. When all members have returned to their original places, the facilitator says: "Now close your eyes and walk the distance to the wall. Be aware of any differences between your present space, distance and location perceptions and those you experienced when you had your eyes open.

When you reach the wall, touch it and explore it. Be aware of any differences between your present exploration perceptions and those you experienced when your eyes were open. When you have finished, rejoin the original group and we will discuss this experience."

Suggestions for Facilitator Process

Concentrate on the following during processing:

a. What feelings and perceptions about space, distance and location did you have when you had your eyes open? How did your perceptions and feelings change when you repeated the exercise with your eyes closed? Why do you think these changes occurred?

b. What feelings and perceptions were stimulated by your wall exploration when your eyes were open? How did your feelings and perceptions change when you explored the wall with your eyes closed? Why do you think these changes occurred?

Variations

Variation I

a. Repeat steps *a* through *d* of the original exercise, but *omit* the last sentence. Replace it with the following: "When you have finished, open your eyes and again find a spot in the room where you feel some degree of privacy. Place yourself the distance from the wall which elicits the most positive feelings about space, distance and location."

b. When all are positioned, repeat the original exercise. During processing concentrate on why members did (or did not) find new locations and why they did (or did not) choose a new distance.

SPATIAL RELATIONS

Subsidiary Goal(s)

a. To explore the dynamics involved in spatial relationships.
b. To gain greater insight into physical surroundings.
c. To examine member relationships.

Group Application

Twelve members or less. To be used with encounter, personal growth, marathon and t-groups.

Application Variables

Twenty minutes. The exercise is 100 per cent non-verbal. The room must be large enough to allow members unrestrained movement.

Administrative Procedure

a. The facilitator gives the following instructions: "I want everyone to silently move about the room. As you are moving, I want you to become aware of the space that you occupy and how you feel about it. When you find a spot that you are extremely comfortable with, I want you to occupy it in any way you feel appropriate."
b. After all members have found a spot and occupied it, the facilitator says: "I want you to become aware of what makes your space a comfortable one. Look around the room. Try to get in touch with the spatial relationships between the members in the group and of your own relationship to the other members. Check out your body *and* your head."
c. After several minutes, the facilitator adds: "When you feel ready I want you to stand up and again start silently moving about the room. This time I would like you to occupy a space that you feel uncomfortable or awkward with."

d. After everyone has assumed a position, the facilitator says: "Get in touch with your feelings about your space. Silently compare it to the first space you occupied. Again look around the room. Become aware of members' positions and of your own. When you feel ready resume your original position in the group circle and we will discuss the experience."

Suggestions for Facilitator Process

Concentrate on the following during processing:

a. What made you feel comfortable with the first space you occupied? What was your relationship to the other members in the group? What other things were you aware of? What feelings occurred within you?

b. What made you feel uncomfortable about the second space you occupied? What was your relationship to other members in the group? Did you try and make your space more comfortable? If so, how? What differences and similarities did you find between your first and second space?

Variations

None

STONE EXPLORATION

Subsidiary Goal(s)

a. To learn that most of us usually use one sense in forming evaluations, judgements and impressions.

b. To become aware of the differences in one's sensory development.

c. To develop insight into one's feelings about giving and receiving.

Group Application

Twenty members or less. Applicable to any group. The exercise is especially valuable when used with t-groups and classroom groups where the facilitator wishes to illustrate that man seldom uses his five senses in forming impressions about such things as beauty and ugliness, goodness and badness, value and worthlessness, etc.

Application Variables

Ten to fifteen minutes. The exercise is 100 per cent non-verbal. An assortment of stones and rocks is needed. The assortment should be large enough so that each member has three or four possible choices.

Administrative Procedure

a. The facilitator places the stone and rock assortment on the floor. He then, if he desires, gives a brief lecturette about how man fails to use all his senses when forming evaluations, judgements and impressions.

b. He says: "Non-verbally, go to the stone assortment and choose a stone. Be aware of the reasons for your choice! When you have chosen your stone, find a place in the room where you feel comfortable and sit down."

c. When all members are seated, the facilitator says: "Let's explore our choices as totally as we can. First, look at your rock. Look at it carefully. Try to see it all. Try not to rely too much on your sense of touch. Just look!"

d. After two or three minutes, he says: "Now, touch your rock. Feel it all over. Feel its being, its texture, its top, bottom, and sides."

e. After two or three minutes, the facilitator continues: "Close your eyes and turn on your ears. Hear how the rock sounds as it contacts your hands, the floor and other objects. Listen to it!"

f. After two or three minutes, the facilitator says: "Taste your rock. Be aware of how it tastes! Does it taste the same all over its surface, or does its taste vary?"

g. After a minute, he says: "Now, smell your rock. Be aware of the rock's odor. Is it the same as you rotate it, or does its smell vary?"

h. After a minute, he continues: "You may now put your stone back or you may keep it. You may give it to someone else if you wish. You may ask another for his stone if you so desire. Do what you wish, then we will discuss this experience."

Suggestions for Facilitator Process

Concentrate on the following during processing:
a. Which sensory exploration was most meaningful? Why? Which exploration did you find most uncomfortable? Why?
b. Which of your senses did you find most highly developed? Which did you find you had difficulty using? Why? What have you learned about how you make use of your senses in forming impressions, opinions, judgments, etc.?
c. Most members will have kept their stone. Ask them why. If any returned the stone, ask them why? Ask why those who gave away stones did so. Ask why those who asked for another member's stone did so.

Variations

None

SUPPORT

Subsidiary Goal(s)

a. To gain further awareness of one's feelings about physical contact.
b. To relieve tension.

Group Application

Twelve members or less. Since dyads are used, group size should be even. To be used with encounter, personal growth, marathon and t-groups. Best results are obtained if the exercise is used at the end of a group session when tension reduction seems advisable.

Application Variables

Thirty minutes. The exercise is 95 per cent non-verbal and 5 per cent verbal. The room should be large enough to allow the dyads unrestrained movement. Candles may be used to enhance the effect.

Administrative Procedure

a. The facilitator asks that dyads be formed. The pairing may be done verbally or non-verbally.

b. When the dyads are formed, the facilitator says: "Remove your shoes and socks. Then find some wall space which you may use to lean upon."

c. When this is done, he says: "One of you is to lean back against the wall. The other is to kneel at your feet."

d. The facilitator says to the leaning members: "Close your eyes. When you feel comfortable, signal your partner."

e. *To the kneelers:* "When you receive your signal, lift one of your partner's feet a few inches above the floor. Do not manipulate, rub or massage it. Simply hold it.

If you sense that your partner needs to rebalance himself, set his foot down and wait for his signal. Then relift the foot.

When you feel that your partner is ready to have his foot placed back on the floor, do so."

f. The facilitator tells the learners: "Try to get in touch with your feelings and sensations. Be aware of how your foot feels about being supported.

When your foot is replaced, take a few moments to savor and feel the experience. Signal your partner when you are ready to have your other foot lifted."

g. After the second lift, the roles are reversed and steps *d* through *f* are repeated.

Suggestions for Facilitator Process

Concentrate on the following during processing:

a. Did you feel support coming from your partner? Did you feel he cared for you? Did you trust him? (To these, ask why and why not, depending on the responses). What feelings and sensations were you aware of as your foot was being supported?

b. Were there differences in feelings and sensations between your feet? If so, in what way? How do you explain this?

c. How did you feel about supporting your partner's foot?

What were your feelings and sensations as you supported his foot? Do you believe you were responsive to your partner's needs? How?

Variations

None

THANKS—I NEEDED THAT

Subsidiary Goal(s)

a. To give and receive feedback.
b. To explore the dynamics involved in touch.

Group Application

Twelve members or less. Since dyads are used, group size should be even. To be used with encounter, personal growth, marathon and t-groups. Best results are obtained if the exercise is used with members who have had previous exposure to sensory awareness.

Application Variables

Twenty minutes. The exercise is 100 per cent non-verbal. The room must be large enough to allow members to spread out without feeling unduly restricted.

Administrative Procedure

a. The facilitator asks members to non-verbally form dyads.
b. Each dyad is told to non-verbally decide which partner will be the first to go through the "receiving" role of the exercise. After this has been decided, the member "receiving" is to lie on his stomach.
c. The facilitator gives the following insructions: "I want the member on the floor to get as comfortable as possible. Your partner will gently, but firmly, begin to slap your shoulders, back, legs, feet, etc. As your partner is slapping you I want you to fully experience the sensations. If your partner is slapping you too gently or with too much force, non-verbally inform him of this. Become aware of your breathing and of

the sections of your body being touched. Concentrate on your feelings, sensations and reactions to the slapping. You will be given approximately ten minutes. Please begin."

d. After ten minutes, the roles are reversed and step *c* is repeated. After all members have completed the exercise, the group processes the experience.

Suggestions for Facilitator Process

Concentrate on the following during processing:

a. *To the members "receiving":* What were your criteria for pairing off? How did you decide which member in your dyad would be the "receiver"? What feelings did you experience while being slapped?

b. *To the members "sending":* When slapping your partner, were you concerned about the intensity of your touch? Did you feel your partner was uncomfortable at any time? When? Why? What else were you aware of while you were touching your partner?

c. *To all:* How do you now feel about your partner? Why do you feel closer to him? Why more distant? What have you learned about yourself and your partner?

Variations

None

*THE BREATH OF LIFE

Subsidiary Goal(s)

a. To explore the dynamics involved in fantasy.
b. To deal with anger, frustration and anxiety.
c. To become more in touch with one's feelings.

Group Application

Twelve members or less. To be used with encounter, personal growth, marathon and t-groups. Best results are obtained if the exercise is used with members who have had extensive exposure to sensory awareness.

Application Variables

Thirty minutes. The exercise is 100 per cent non-verbal. The room must be large enough to allow members to spread out without feeling unduly restricted.

Administrative Procedure

a. The facilitator gives the following introduction: "Breathing is an extremely important function of our body. Yet, we often take it for granted. Awareness of our breathing can often give us greater insight into our feelings and thoughts.

I would like you to spread out within the room. Please remain standing with your eyes closed." For heightening of effect, a darkened room lit by candlelight is recommended.

b. After all members have positioned themselves within the room, the facilitator says: "Begin to breathe slowly and deeply. Let your entire body flow with the motion of your breathing. In and out, in and out. Let your arms hang loose. Let your head slowly rock."

c. After several minutes, he continues: "Begin to think of a situation in which you were very frustrated. Let yourself experience that frustration. Notice your breathing. Let your body, feelings and thoughts follow your breathing pattern."

d. After several more minutes, he adds: "Now, begin to feel anxious. Let yourself relive an experience in which you were scared. Feel your tenseness. Let your body flow with what you are experiencing. Again become aware of your breathing. Pay attention to how your fears affect it."

e. When the facilitator feels that members have truly reached a point of experiencing anxiety, he states: "Become angry! Let yourself experience the stored up anger and hostility you have been carrying around with you. Begin to pant, let your body tense. Get in touch with your anger. Feel the anger. Experience the anger. Feel and be aware of your breathing and your body."

f. After several minutes, he says: "Slowly let your anger subside. It is almost as if you have a pressure valve. Open the valve and let the anger dissipate.

Now that you have let out some steam, you can begin to feel good spaces within yourselves, spaces without so much pressure. Slowly begin to get comfortable. Let your body begin to relax. Start breathing slowly and deeper. When you feel really comfortable, open your eyes and rejoin the group for processing. Please take your time."

Suggestions for Facilitator Process

Concentrate on the following during processing:

a. How did your breathing differ through your experiences in the exercise? Did you actually become frustrated, anxious and angry? If not, why not? Were any of these emotions more difficult to achieve than another? Which ones and why?
b. Were you able to let your body follow your breathing? If so, how did you accomplish this? Were there any experiences which you relived which you would like to share with the group?
c. What have you learned about dealing with your emotions? Do you feel you actually relieved some pressure within you? What is your breathing like right now?

Variations

None

THERE I ARE[4]

Subsidiary Goal(s)

a. To develop awareness of oneself as a physical being.
b. To experience frustration.

Group Application

Twelve members or less. Since dyads are used, group size should be even. Applicable to any group.

Application Variables

Ten minutes. The exercise is 60 per cent non-verbal and 40 per cent verbal. A full length mirror for each dyad is required. The

---

[4]Adapted from an exercise developed by Dan Millar, Coordinator of Interpersonal and Public Communication, Central Michigan University.

room must be large enough to insure that reflections from other dyads will not appear in any dyad's mirror.

Administrative Procedure

a. The facilitator asks that dyads be formed. He says: "Non-verbally decide who will be the sender and who the receiver."

b. After step *a* has been completed, the facilitator gives one mirror to each dyad. He says: "Spread out in the room. The receiver is to hold the mirror in such a manner that the sender sees himself only. No part of the receiver is to be visible. Nor should other dyads' reflections be visible to the sender." (Handles or wires fastened firmly to the back of the mirror are helpful.)

c. The facilitator tells the senders: "Look at your reflections. Try to become aware of the totality of your image."

d. After three minutes, the facilitator says: "Initiate a conversation with the receiver. Find a topic on which the two of you disagree. Try to determine the extent and intensity of the disagreement."

e. After two minutes, roles are reversed and steps *c* and *d* are repeated.

Suggestions for Facilitator Process

Concentrate on the following during processing:

a. *To senders:* Did you look away from your image? When? Why? What were your feet, legs and torso doing? Did you feel frustrated during the conversation? Why? Did your partner's voice grow in importance as the conversation advanced?

b. *To receivers:* How did you feel during the experience? What body reactions were you aware of? Did you experience any frustration? When? How did you cope with it?

c. *To all:* Which was most enjoyable and meaningful, sending or receiving? Why? What have you learned about yourself as a sender and receiver in communication situations?

Variations

Variation I

a. Give a full or half-length mirror to each member.

b. Then have the members spread out and read poetry to their mirror images. The poetry should cover diverse topics and express differing emotional states. (For example, sexual love, fear, faith in a God, and loneliness are possible topic areas.)

c. Tell the members to watch themselves as they read and to become aware of their internal feelings and their body reactions.

*THROUGH THE LOOKING GLASS

Subsidiary Goal(s)

a. To explore the dynamics involved in non-verbal feedback.

b. To gain further insight into images and impressions.

Group Application

Twelve members or less. Since dyads are used, group size should be even. To be used with encounter, personal growth, marathon and t-groups. Best results are obtained if the exercise is used in the middle of the group's life.

Application Variables

Thirty minutes. The exercise is 100 per cent non-verbal. The room should be large enough to allow members to spread out unrestrained.

Administrative Procedure

a. The facilitator asks members to mill around non-verbally and pair off with another member. The dyads are to find a semi-private spot in the room and stand facing each other.

b. He then asks the members to stand perfectly straight and to maintain constant eye contact.

c. The facilitator then gives the following instructions: "I would like you to copy your partner's facial expression and body position as accurately as possible. Try to become aware of your physical position as it relates to your partner's physical position."

d. After both members have mirrored one another, the facilitator tells the members to loosen their bodies, close their eyes and let their body reform its own identity.

e. After a few minutes the members are asked to regroup and repeat the process with a different partner.

f. Steps *a* through *d* are repeated.

Suggestions for Facilitator Process

Concentrate on the following during processing:

a. Why did you pair off with the members you did? What type of feedback did you receive from your partner? Was it accurate? What types of feedback did you try to express? Was it perceived accurately?

b. How did you feel while maintaining constant eye contact? What part of your body were you aware of? What have you learned about the way in which you are being perceived? Did both of your partners give you the same feedback?

Variations

None

UNLOOSENING EYES #1

Subsidiary Goal(s)

a. To learn how one's vision can be restricted due to muscle tension in or around the eyes.

b. To learn that one can control how much or how little he allows himself to see.

Group Application

Group size is unlimited. However, if processing is to occur, the group size should be twenty or less. Applicable to any group.

Application Variables

Five to ten minutes. The exercise is 100 per cent non-verbal.

Administrative Procedure

a. The facilitator gives a brief lecturette about the manner in which vision can be restricted by bodily tensions, cultural learnings, and self-concept.

b. He then says: "Let's do a few exercises which can help us loosen our vision. First, smile as broadly as you can. Now, look down with your eyes. Do not move your head. Be aware of what you can see."

c. After five or ten seconds, he says: "Stop smiling. Now look down. Be aware of what you can see. The difference in visions is enormous."

d. After five or ten seconds, he says: "Now, hold your hand about ten inches from your face. Study your hand. Really look at it! Don't let anything else interfere with your hand observation."

e. After one or two minutes, he says: "Keep your hand where it is, but try your best to ignore it. Without moving your eyes from your hand, become aware of all the other things you are, and have been, seeing."

f. After one or two minutes, the facilitator continues: "Lie down on your back. Open your eyes wide. Move your eyes as far right as you can, then down, then left, then up. Breathing evenly and deeply, repeat this movement five times."

g. After five seconds, he says: "Reverse the order. Move your eyes as far left as you can, then up, then right, then down. Repeat this five times, then we will discuss this experience."

Suggestions for Facilitator Process

Concentrate on the following during processing:

a. How do your face and eye muscles feel now? It there less tension? Why is this so?

b. Do you think these exercises increased your ability to see? If yes, why? If no, why not?

c. When you concentrated on your hand, did you have difficulty ignoring other stimuli? Why? When you were told to ignore your hand, were you able to do so? If not, why not? If yes, what were you able to see?

Variations

None

UNLOOSENING EYES #2

Subsidiary Goal(s)

a. To learn how one has a tendency to overfocus on one item in the field of view.

b. To learn to become aware of peripheral stimuli and background detail.

Group Application

Group size is unlimited. However, if processing is to occur, the group size should be twenty or less. Applicable to any group.

Application Variables

Five to ten minutes. The exercise is 100 per cent non-verbal. Access to the outdoors is needed. The outdoor scenery should be full of visual stimuli, e.g., trees, rocks, buildings, people, etc.

Administrative Procedure

a. The facilitator gives a brief lecturette about how man spends most of his time staring and looking and little of his time *seeing*.

b. He then says: "Let's go outside and unloosen our vision."

c. When the group is outside and the members are comfortably situated, the facilitator says: "Cross your eyes for five or ten seconds, then relax them by closing your eyes and gently massaging your eyelids. Massage them until your eyes feel relaxed and your eye muscles feel less tense."

d. When all members are ready, he continues: "Crossing your eyes makes it evident what it's like to overfocus. Now, look off into the distance. Just look."

e. After thirty seconds, he says: "Become aware of what you're looking at. I say that because I bet you are looking at and focusing on some thing, instead of really seeing all the things that are in your field of vision." Pausing brieflly, he continues: "Now, try to see what is there. Try not to focus on any one thing."

f. After two or three minutes, the facilitator stops the group and has them discuss the experience.

Suggestions for Facilitator Process

Concentrate on the following during processing:

a. Do you feel you learned about the differences between staring and focusing versus seeing? What are the differences that you are now aware of?

b. Was I right when I said you were looking at something rather than seeing? To those who say yes, ask them what they were focusing on and why. Then ask, after I asked you to "see what is there," did you still focus and look at things? Most will say no. Ask them what they saw.

c. Which is easier, focusing or seeing? Why? Which do you prefer, to focus or to see? Why?

Variations

None

VIBRATIONS

Subsidiary Goal(s)

a. To localize physical sensations.
b. To explore the dynamics in trust.
c. To explore one's feelings about physical contact.

Group Application

Twelve members or less. Since dyads are used, group size should be even. To be used with encounter, personal growth, marathon and t-groups.

Application Variables

Thirty minutes. The exercise is 95 per cent non-verbal and 5 per cent verbal. The room should be large enough to allow the members to spread out comfortably.

Administrative Procedure

a. The facilitator asks that dyads be formed. This can be done verbally or non-verbally.

b. He then says to the dyads: "Spread out within the room. Find a place where the two of you feel comfortable."

c. When this is accomplished, he continues: "One of you is to stand facing your partner's shoulder so that the dyad, if looked at from above, resembles a "T." I will illustrate this if you do not understand." (If illustration is required, the facilitator should then do so.).

d. He then says to the "shoulder-facing" members: "Place one hand upon the top of your partner's forehead and the other upon the base of his skull. Do not manipulate, rub or massage the contact areas. Do, however, try to let the feelings or "vibrations" you have for your partner flow through your fingers and into him."

e. He says to the members who are being touched: "Close your eyes and try to pick up the vibrations. When you feel that you have received enough physical contact, signal your partner. The signal is to be given non-verbally. Your partner will then remove his hands from your forehead and skull."

f. After all dyads are finished, the facilitator says: "Those of you facing your partner's shoulders are now to place one hand on his throat and the other upon the base of his skull. Try to send him your feelings and "vibrations" without manipulating your hand."

g. As before, the member receiving the contact is told to non-verbally indicate when he wants his partner to release the contact.

h. After all dyads are finished, he continues: "Now, those of you who have been touching your partner, place one hand upon your partner's upper chest and the other on his back. When you receive your non-verbal signal, break the contact."

i. When all dyads are finished, the facilitator tells the "touched" members to take a few minutes to absorb and reflect on the experience. Roles are then reversed and steps *c* through *h* are repeated.

Suggestions for Facilitator Process

Concentrate on the following during processing:

a. *To the members being touched:* What feelings and sensa-

Figure 8-9. Vibrations

tons did you experience when you were touched? How did
these differ through the three touching stages? Why? Was
your partner responsive to your needs? What feelings and
"vibrations" did you pick up?

b. *To the members who touched:* How did you feel about
touching your partner? Were you tense? When and why?
Were you anxious? When and why? Did your feelings about
touching vary through the three stages? If so, how and why?

c. *To all:* What have you learned about your body? What have
you learned about your feelings about touching and being
touched?

Variations

None

WALLPAPERING

Subsidiary Goal(s)

a. To develop awareness of body space.
b. To learn how to cope with invasion of private space.

Group Application

Group size is unlimited and is limited only by room size. However, the Wallpapering exercise is most easily utilized with
groups of twenty or less. Applicable to any group, but most
commonly used with encounter, personal growth, marathon and
t-groups.

Application Variables

Ten to fifteen minutes. The exercise is 100 per cent non-verbal.
The room must be small enough to allow the members to wallpaper it with their bodies. (See Administrative Procedure for
an explanation of the wallpapering concept) . If the room is too
large, wallpaper one or two walls. If it is unduly large, use
Variation I.

Administrative Procedure

a. The facilitator says: "Non-verbally, go to the walls of the
room and wallpaper it with your body. Stand with your back

to the wall and your shoulders and thighs touching your neighbors."

b. If the room is too large, tell the members to wallpaper one (or two if necessary) wall.

c. After the members are lined up, shoulders and thighs touching each other, the facilitator says: "Close your eyes. Get in touch with your feelings about where you are."

d. After two or three minutes he says: "Now, tune your feelings to your neighbors. How do they feel? How do you feel?"

e. After two or three minutes he continues: "Turn and face the wall, still touching shoulders and thighs. Now, concentrate on how you feel. What are the differences in your feelings? Tune in on them and experience them."

f. After two or three minutes the facilitator says: "Now, tune your feelings to your neighbors. How do they feel now? How do you feel now?"

g. After two or three minutes the facilitator says: "Spread out the wallpaper so you are no longer touching each other. Now tune into and experience your feelings."

h. After two or three minutes the group stops and discusses the experience.

Suggestions for Facilitator Process

Concentrate on the following during processing:

a. How did you feel during the varying stages of the exercise? How did your feelings vary from stage one, where your backs were to the wall, to stage two, where you faced the wall, to stage three, where you had unencumbered space? Why was this so?

b. Did you feel closed in? Why? What did you feel about your neighbors as their bodies touched you? Any difference in feelings for them when you turned and faced the wall? Why?

c. Which stage did you like the most? Why? Which stage did you dislike the most? Why? What have you learned about space and infringement of private space?

Variations

Variation I

a. If the room is so large that one wall cannot be wallpapered, have the group form a circle. They are to touch shoulders and thighs, but are *not* to encircle each other's waists with their arms.

b. Repeat step *c* through *h* of the original exercise.

*WOMB CARRY

Subsidiary Goal(s)

a. To develop group unity.

b. To encourage participation.

Group Application

Twelve members or less. To be used with encounter, personal growth, marathon and t-groups. Best used after the members have met for a long enough period of time for care, trust and warmth to have developed between them.

Application Variables

Two to five minutes per participant. The exercise is 100 per cent non-verbal. A darkened room lit only by candles will enhance the effect.

Administrative Procedure

a. The facilitator says: "I would like a volunteer who is willing to experience birth."

b. The volunteer is told: "Lie on the floor and assume the prenatal position. Curl up tight and become a fetus."

c. He tells the others: "We are going to become a human womb and carry the fetus. Half of you place your arms under the fetus and lift it up. The others use your arms and bodies to enclose the fetus."

d. When step *c* has been accomplished, the facilitator says: "Let's carry the fetus." He says to the volunteer: "Try to become a fetus. Be aware of your reactions and feelings to being carried in the womb."

e. After a few minutes, the facilitator stops the womb carry and says: "Stand still." He tells the volunteer: "You are about to be born. Come out of the womb. Be born."

f. After the birth, processing should occur. Then, all others who wish to experience the womb carry should be given the opportunity to do so.

Suggestions for Facilitator Process

Concentrate on the following during processing:

a. *To the volunteer:* How did you feel during the carry? Did you feel warm, secure and safe? If no, why not? Which did you enjoy the most, being carried or being born? Why? Explore the volunteer's reasons for his method of birth. For example, did he emerge at one of the ends of the womb? Did he emerge wiggling, crying, screaming or silently?

b. *To the others:* How did you feel during the experience? Why did you (or did you not) volunteer to be carried? Did you enjoy carrying the fetus more than giving it birth? Why? Why not?

Variations

None

IX

TRUST

THE PRIMARY GOAL for each exercise in this chapter is the exploration of trust.

Trust is one of the most basic dynamics involved in interpersonal growth. The potential value of the following exercises cannot be overstressed. The facilitator should bear in mind that expression of trust assumes many forms. Several dynamics such as self-disclosure, risk-taking, feedback and even anger are intricately interwoven in the development of trust. The following exercises are not designed to artifically create trust, but rather to explore the level of trust at a particular moment in the group's life.

We believe that the accurate assessment of trust provides input which furthers both the group's and individual's development. It is our experience that the appropriate use of trust exercises can heighten and expand upon already existing feelings. However we do suggest that the facilitator give careful consideration to both the selection and processing of trust exercises.

BODY TRUST

Subsidiary Goal(s)

a. To learn how to concentrate on feelings instead of thoughts.
b. To develop warmth between members.

Group Application

Twelve members or less. To be used with encounter, personal growth, marathon and t-groups whose members have had sufficient sessions to have developed warmth and care for each other.

Application Variables

One to two minutes per member being "swung." (See Administrative Procedure, step *d.*) The exercise is 100 per cent nonverbal.

245

Administrative Procedure

a. Whenever the facilitator notices that a member appears to be uncertain about how much he can trust others or is trusted by them, he says to the member: "You appear really uncertain as to how much you can trust us. Let's do something non-verbally which will help you decide."

b. He tells the member: "Lie on the floor with your arms and legs spread."

c. He then tells the member: "Look around and non-verbally indicate four members you feel little trust for."

d. When the four members have been designated, the facilitator tells them: "Go to the member. Take his arms and legs and do with him what you will.

Swing him, throw him between you, pull him. Do to him what you wish. When you feel you are finished, set him down. We will then discuss the experience."

e. After processing, any other members who wish the experience are given the opportunity to do so.

Suggestions for Facilitator Process

Concentrate on the following during processing:

a. *To the member(s) swung:* How did you feel during the swing? How do you feel now? Do you trust the group more? If yes, why? If no, why not?

b. *To the swingers:* How did you feel during the swinging exercise? Do you feel warmer or more trusting to the member? If yes, why? If no, why not?

c. *To others:* What did you see going on? Did the swinger appear to trust the foursome? If yes, how? If no, how did he deny trust?

Variations

None

*FALLING

Subsidiary Goal(s)

a. To encourage risk taking behavior.

Group Application

Twelve members or less. To be used with encounter, personal growth, marathon and t-groups. This is an excellent exercise to use with groups whose members are hesitant with regard to testing their trust level, as it is relatively safe.

Application Variables

Two to three minutes per participant. The exercise is 100 per cent non-verbal.

Administrative Procedure

a. The facilitator makes the following statement: "This exercise is designed to let us explore our level of trust for the group. I would like a volunteer to enter the middle of the circle."

b. After a volunteer has entered the middle of the circle, the facilitator instructs the group to stand up and form a closely knit circle around the volunteer. The facilitator says to the volunteer: "When I say begin I want you to close your eyes and let yourself fall. The members in the circle will catch you and stand you back up so you may let yourself fall again. Try and keep your feet planted in the middle of the circle. When you feel you have had enough, simply open your eyes and rejoin the circle."

c. After the volunteer has rejoined the circle, another volunteer is asked for until all members have had an opportunity to be in the center of the circle. When completed, the group rejoins for processing.

Suggestions for Facilitator Process

Concentrate on the following during processing:

a. *To the members in the center of the circle:* What sensations did you have while falling? Were there any doubts as to whether or not you would be caught? Why? Why not? Was your body relaxed or tense? Was it difficult keeping your eyes closed? How much do you feel you trusted the group?

b. *To the members in the outer circle:* How much responsibility did you feel for the member falling? What were you aware of during this time? How did you perceive the other members in the circle? Do you feel the member falling trusted the group? If not, why?

Variations

None

*LIFT AND ROCK

Subsidiary Goal(s)

    a. To encourage risk taking behavior.
    b. To increase sensory awareness.

Group Application

Twelve members or less. To be used with encounter, personal growth, marathon and t-groups. Best results will occur if the exercise is used after an initial climate of trust has developed, Caution should be used if the exercise is prematurely applied.

Application Variables

Two to three minutes per participant. The exercise is 100 per cent non-verbal. The optimal environment is a large, spacious outdoor setting. If conducted inside, the room must be large enough to allow the group unrestricted movement.

Administrative Procedure

    a. The facilitator makes the following statement: "The exploration of our feelings of trust is an extremely important dynamic to consider. This exercise is designed to allow us to experience trust in terms of dependency on the group."
    b. The facilitator asks for a volunteer who is willing to test his trust of the group.
    c. The volunteer is told to enter the circle. The facilitator then says: "When I say begin, I would like you to let yourself fall. The other members in the group will support you. The group will then lift you above their heads, hold you there and then slowly rock you. At that point I want you to try

and let your entire body relax and become solely dependent upon the group for support. There is to be no talking and please keep your eyes closed during the entire experience. Please begin."

d. After the member has been held in the air for a few minutes, the facilitator tells the group: "Slowly lower the member to

Figure 9-1. Lift and Rock

waist level. Now begin rocking the member slowly. "
e. After the group has rocked the member for several minutes he/she is slowly lowered on to the floor. The facilitator says to the volunteer: "Before you arise take time to digest the experience. Let yourself absorb as many sensations as possible."
f. After all who wish the experience have done so, the members discuss the exercise.

Suggestions for Facilitator Process

Concentrate on the following during processing:

a. *To the members being lifted and rocked:* What was your initial reaction to leaning back and letting the group support your weight? What were you aware of while being held in the air?
b. What sensation did you experience while being rocked? Did you find it difficult keeping your eyes closed? How much do you feel you now trust the group? Has it changed because of this experience? If so, in what way? Why?
c. *To the member's lifting and rocking:* What were you aware of while lifting and rocking the member? Do you feel you supported more or less than your share of the member's weight? How gentle or rough did you perceive yourself and others being during the exercise.

Variations

Variation I

a. Repeat the original exercise.
b. Then, repeat the lift and rock, but have the volunteer keep his eyes open.
c. During processing, determine what, if any, feeling and sensation differences occurred.

*NET TOSS

Subsidiary Goal(s)

a. To learn how one feels about having his safety depend on others.

Group Application

Twelve members or less. To be used with encounter, personal growth, marathon and t-groups. The exercise can be used, with caution, with classroom groups who wish to investigate the phenomenon of trust. The exercise should be conducted after the group has met a period of time sufficent for beginning trust to have developed.

Application Variables

Two to three minutes per participant. The exercise is 100 per cent non-verbal. A strong and sturdy fisherman's net is needed. (A blanket may be used, but many trust dynamics will be voided by such a substitution.). The exercise should be conducted outdoors. If it is conducted indoors, the ceiling of the room must be high enough to insure the safety of the individual being tossed.

Administrative Procedure

a. The facilitator says: "We are now at a stage where we are beginning to trust each other. Let's see if we can't strengthen that trust.
   I have a very strong net (or blanket). Who will volunteer to trust us to toss him in the net?"

b. The volunteer is told to lie down on the net. All other members grab hold of the net. The facilitator then says: "We will toss you. We will *not* let go of the net or let you fall from it."

c. The members then toss the volunteer. The facilitator will find that, at first, most volunteers will hold onto the netting. As they grow in trust, they will let go of the netting and allow their body to bounce upward. This pre-trust holding is the *big advantage* for using a net. A blanket does not allow one to "save" himself by holding on.

d. After the volunteer has been tossed enough that it is evident he *trusts* the group, a new volunteer is sought. The exercise is repeated until all who wish to be "tossed" have had the opportunity to do so.

Suggestions for Facilitator Process

Concentrate on the following during processing:

a. *To those who were tossed:* Were you aware that you held onto the netting? What do you think this signified? Did you, eventually, let go? What do you think that meant about your trust level? How did you feel during the toss? How do you feel now? Do you trust us? If yes, why? If no, why not?

b. *To the tossers:* How did you feel as you tossed others? How did your feelings differ from one toss to another? How do you explain these differences?

c. If any did not let themselves be tossed, ask them why and how they now feel about the net toss and their part in it.

Variations

*Variation I

a. To be used only after a good deal of trust has developed. To heighten the experience for all, blindfold the volunteer and *all but one* of the tossers.

b. The facilitator then says: "You (name the seeing member) are to guide us as we toss (name the volunteer). We will have to trust you to insure the safety of the volunteer."

c. All who wish to participate are given the opportunity to do so. During processing, concentrate on the feelings of the sighted and unsighted members.

*NON-VERBAL TRUST WALK[1]

Subsidiary Goal(s)

a. To gain greater awareness of physical surroundings.
b. To enhance and explore non-verbal communication.
c. To examine and enhance member relationships.
d. To increase sensory awareness.

---

[1]Although the trust walk has traditionally been seen as an exercise in trust, the authors have found, when they use it, that the increase in sensory awareness factor is equally important. Therefore, the facilitator should feel free to use this exercise when increasing sensory awareness is his primary goal.

Group Application

Twenty members or less. If processing is to be done, the group size should be twelve or less. Since dyads are used, group size should be even. Applicable to any group, but most frequently used with encounter, personal growth, marathon and t-groups. This exercise is quite effective when used with classroom groups who are studying trust and/or sensory awareness. As a trust exercise, best results are obtained if the exercise is used *before* extensive trust has been established between the members. As a sensory awareness exercise (see footnote), best results are obtained if it is used *after* extensive trust has been established between the members.

Application Variables

One to one and a half hours. The exercise is 100 per cent non-verbal. An outdoor environment in which there is a great deal of space and a multitude of objects to be explored is desired. A park with a playground is ideal. Blindfolds sufficient to outfit the number of dyads are needed.

Administrative Procedure

a. The facilitator asks the members to non-verbally mill around and form dyads with someone they have neutral or negative feelings for.

b. Each dyad is given a blindfold and told: "Decide who will be blindfolded first. You are going on a trust walk and your partner will lead you."

c. After one member of each dyad is blindfolded, the facilitator tells the members: "When you are the seeing member, you have fifteen minutes to lead your partner around the area. Let him depend on you. Try to lead him over, through, under, and around things and places. Get him to explore by helping him smell, touch, hear and taste things. After fifteen minutes, switch roles."

d. After all members are back, the facilitator says: "Now, non-verbally mill and choose a partner for whom you have positive and warm feelings."

e. Step *b* and *c* are repeated.

f. After all are back, the members discuss the experience.

Suggestions for Facilitator Process

Concentrate on the following during processing:

a. *To the first dyads:* Have your feelings changed toward your partner? In what way? Why? What did you discover about your surroundings? What are you aware of now which you were not previously aware of? What have you learned about yourself? Did you enjoy leading or being led? Why?

b. *To the second dyads:* Have your feelings changed toward your partner? How did the second experience differ from the first? Why?

c. *To all:* Do you feel you risked? How? Was the experience a valuable one for you? Why? Why not?

Variations

None

*TRUST JUMP

Subsidiary Goal(s)

a. To encourage risk taking behavior.

Group Application

Twelve members or less. To be used with encounter, personal growth, marathon and t-groups *after* a climate of trust has been developed.

Application Variables

Seven to ten minutes. The exercise is 100 per cent non-verbal. An outdoor setting is most ideal. The outdoor setting *must* have little hills and knolls which can be used for jumping purposes. If conducted indoors, small stools or chairs are needed in a *carpeted* room.

Administrative Procedure

a. The facilitator gives the following instructions: "Mill around non-verbally and pair off with two other members towards whom you feel a high level of trust."

b. After all triads have formed, the facilitator passes out one blindfold to each. The facilitator then states: "When I say begin, decide non-verbally among you who will be blindfolded first. The member blindfolded is to be led by the other two members in the triad to a point from which he/she may jump. (If outdoors a small slope is sufficient. If within a room a chair may be used.) The apex should be no more than three feet from the ground. When you jump the other two members in your triad are to catch you. If you have strong reservations about participation please refrain." The facilitator now asks the members to begin. (It should be suggested to triads in which one member is substantially larger than the other two, that the point from which they jump should be closer to the ground.)

c. After all triads have completed the trust jump, the subgroups rejoin for processing.

Suggestions for Facilitator Process

Concentrate on the following during processing:

a. How did you non-verbally decide who would be the first to jump? Do you feel the member jumping trusted the other two members in the triad? What are your criteria for this response?

b. What sensations did you have while jumping? Were there any doubts that you would be caught? Did you feel responsible for the member jumping? What were you aware of while waiting for the members in your triad to jump?

c. Who decided how far the members in your triads would jump? Have your feelings changed towards any members in your triad? If so, in what way and why?

Variations

None

X

UNGROUPED EXERCISES

THE EXERCISES in this chapter are our version of the "grab bag." Each has a specific goal (in the upper right-hand corner). However, there is not a sufficient amount of exercises in any goal category to warrant an entire chapter.

We wish to urge the reader to be aware that these exercises are equally as beneficial to groups as are those included in the previous chapters. Do not overlook them.

Creativity

DO YOUR OWN THING

Subsidiary Goal(s)

a. To explore the dynamics of leadership.
b. To experience anxiety and confusion.

Group Application

Twelve members or less. To be used with encounter, personal growth, marathon and t-groups only after the members have met for a sufficient period of time for group unity to have developed. Groups whose members have had considerable previous exposure to non-verbal experiences will benefit most from this exercise.

Application Variables

Half an hour. The exercise is 100 per cent non-verbal.

Administrative Procedure

a. The facilitator says: "We have had previous exposure to non-verbal exercises. However, I usually introduced and conducted them. Today, you are going to create the experience.

You have thirty minutes. Decide, non-verbally, what you want to do. Then, do it."

b. After thirty minutes, the members discuss the experience.

Suggestions for Facilitator Process

Concentrate on the following during processing:

a. Who were the leaders? What did they do to earn those positions? Did you feel anxious, uneasy, or confused at any time? When? How did you cope with these feelings?

b. How did you decide on what non-verbal experience we would have? What was the goal and meaning of your exercise? Did it involve physical contact? Why? Why not?

c. Did your exercise encourage participation by all? How? Why not? What have you learned about yourself and other members?

Variations

None

*CHANGE OF PACE

Subsidiary Goal(s)

a. To explore the dynamics involved in spatial relationships.

b. To gain greater insight into members' perceptions.

c. To give and receive feedback.

d. To explore the dynamics involved in competition.

Group Application

Twelve members or less. To be used with encounter, personal growth, marathon and t-groups. The exercise is designed to be used with groups which have met in the same room over a period of time.

Application Variables

One hour. The exercise is 100 per cent non-verbal. The following items are needed: streamers, construction paper, crayons, colored light bulbs, candles, pillows, blankets and aluminum foil.

Administrative Procedure

a. The facilitator says: "We have been meeting in the same room for a period of time. Many psychologists believe that changing one's environment will affect one's behavior. As you can see, I have brought a variety of items with me. I would like us to change this room by utilizing our imagination and creativity. The group is to non-verbally split into two separate subgroups."

b. After the group has divided itself in half, the following instructions are given: "Each of the subgroups is to be in charge of remodeling one-half of the room. The subgroups must decide non-verbally how the room is to be divided up, how to ration out the limited number of items available and how your subgroup will work in unity to achieve the desired changes in the atmosphere of the room. You will be given forty-five minutes to complete the task. Please begin."

c. After forty-five minutes, the members are told: "Look at our new room. Explore it. Determine your feelings and reactions to its "newness." We will discuss this experience after we have sufficiently explored the room."

Suggestions for Facilitator Process

Concentrate on the following during processing:

a. *To the entire group:* What criteria did you use to pair off non-verbally? Do you feel you were one of the first or last to be included in a subgroup?

b. *To subgroups:* How did you non-verbally divide the room up? Who was the leader? Who were the followers? How did you divide up the items to be used by your subgroup? Did you feel any sense of competition? If so, in what way?

c. *To subgroups:* How did you achieve unity within your subgroup? Were you pleased with the results? If not, why? How did you communicate within your subgroups? Looking around us, what do you feel the environment is now saying to us? What differences do you perceive between the two environments? Which do you feel more comfortable with and why?

Variations

None

*GIFTS

Subsidiary Goal(s)

a. To give and receive feedback.

b. To gain insight into members' perceptions.

c. To give members an opportunity to deal with the dynamics of saying goodbye and to facilitate the closure process.

Group Application

Twelve members or less. To be used with encounter, personal growth, marathon and t-groups. The exercise is designed to be used during the last session of the group's life. In the case of a marathon group, the exercise should be used within the last two hours of the session. The room must be large enough to allow the members to spread out without feeling unduly restricted.

Application Variables

One hour and thirty minutes. The exercise is 50 per cent non-verbal and 50 per cent verbal. The following items are required: Construction paper, crayons, glue, rocks, tissue paper, assorted magazines, scissors, styrofoam balls, rubber bands, magic markers (in assorted colors), felt, glitter, a number of boxes of various sizes, leaves, flowers, rags, plastic baggies, shaving cream, oranges and toothpicks. (A number of other items may be added or substituted according to the availability of the material. In any case a wide variety and number of objects must be present for the exercise.)

Administrative Procedure

a. The facilitator places all the objects in the middle of the circle and gives the following introduction: "As you can see, we have a curious number and assortment of items before us.

We will be saying goodbye soon and it may be very meaningful for each one of us to say goodbye through the use of our
creative resources.

You will have the next forty-five minutes to create a gift for
the group from the items before us. Each member is to work
alone, non-verbally. Feel free to let your imagination run
wild. Create whatever you feel respresents your feeling
toward what the group has been and is. There is enough
material for everyone.

When you are through using a magic marker, crayons, glue,
etc., please return it to the large pile so other members may
use it. You may spread out anywhere you wish to achieve
privacy. I will tell you when the time has elasped. Please
begin."

b. After forty-five minutes, the facilitator tells the members to
rejoin the circle with their objects. (If the gifts are too deli-
cate to be picked up, they may be left on the floor.) The
facilitator states: "Please place your gift in front of you. One
member at a time is to share the meaning of his object and
how it relates to the group."

c. After all members have participated, the group discusses
the experience and its meaning for them.

Suggestions for Facilitator Process

Concentrate on the following during processing:

a. Were you surprised at any of the members' gifts? If so,
whose and why? What type of feedback seemed to be con-
sistant? Did anyone's feedback surprise you? Whose and why?

b. How did you decide what to make? Was it spontaneous or
planned? Do you feel your final gift represented your feelings?
Did saying goodbye through gifts make this unpleasant task
any easier? Why? Why not?

Variations

None

*GROUP POETRY

Subsidiary Goal(s)
    a. To give and receive feedback.
    b. To determine members' perceptions of the group.

Group Application
Twelve members or less. To be used with encounter, personal growth, marathon and t-groups. Best results are obtained if the exercise is conducted during the latter stages of the group's life.

Application Variables
Ten to twenty minutes. The exercise is 90 per cent non-verbal and 10 per cent verbal. One piece of paper and one pencil are needed.

Administrative Procedure
    a. The facilitator says: "We have been together quite a while and have experienced many things. Let's take the opportunity to work together to describe ourselves.

    I have a pencil and paper. I will give them to one of you. That person is to write the *first* line of a poem which describes our group. He then gives the pencil and paper to another member. That member writes the second line. This process will continue until each of us has added a line to the poem."

    b. The facilitator gives the material to any member of his choice. We *do not* recommend that the facilitator start the poem. This can bias the creation. It is best that he take his turn somewhere in the middle of the process and allow members to start and finish the poem.

    c. When the poem is finished, the facilitator (or a member) reads it to the group. The members then discuss the poem and the overall experience.

Suggestions for Facilitator Process

Concentrate on the following during processing:

a. What does our poem tell us about how we perceive the group and ourselves? Does it accurately portray your feelings and perceptions? How? How does it fail to portray your feelings and perceptions?

b. Whose names were mentioned? Why? What group life events were mentioned? Why? How would you change the poem? Why?

Variations

*Variation I

a. Break the group into triads or quartets.

b. Have each member of the subgroups write two lines of poetry.

c. Have all poems read. Then have the group non-verbally reach group consensus as to which subgroup's poem best portrays the group.

d. During processing concentrate on how the aura of competition affected the creative process, how the subgroup members interacted and what criteria were used during the consensus seeking phase.

Feelings

EMOTIONS

Subsidiary Goal(s)

a. To gain greater awareness of one's emotions.

b. To provide one with an opportunity to experience one's body.

Group Application

Twelve members or less. To be used with encounter, personal growth, marathon and t-groups. Best results are obtained if the exercise is used after the group has had ample sessions to allow for the lessening of inhibitions.

Application Variables

Forty-five minutes. The exercise is 100 per cent non-verbal. The room should be large enough to allow members to spread out. A darkened room lighted only by candles will enhance the experience and is highly recommended.

Administrative Procedure

a. The facilitator may wish to present a brief lecturette on the importance of being in touch with one's feelings and emotions.

b. He then asks the members to spread out within the room and to close their eyes.

c. The facilitator then says: "I am going to say an emotion. Keeping your eyes closed I want you to non-verbally express that emotion. Try to pay very close attention to your bodily functions as you express these emotions. You should feel free to move any part of your body, although your eyes are to remain closed. Try not to act out the emotion. However, do try to *experience* and *feel* it."

d. At five minute intervals the facilitator verbally gives the following emotions: disgust, sensuality, anger, hate, care, love, joy and elation.

e. After the members have had a few minutes to absorb the experience, the group discusses the experience.

Suggestions for Facilitator Process

Concentrate on the following during processing:

a. Was it difficult for you to experience the emotions? Why? Were some emotions more difficult to express than others? Which ones and why? What were you aware of during (name one of the emotions)? Continue the last question until all the emotions used have been discussed.

b. What was going on in your body? Do you feel you are better in touch with your emotions? Why? Why not? What awareness, if any, have you discovered within yourself?

Variations

None

*FEEDBACK

Subsidiary Goal(s)

    a. To experience communication on a non-verbal level.

    b. To give and receive feedback.

    c. To explore the dynamics involved in confrontation.

Group Application

    Twelve members or less. To be used with encounter, personal growth, marathon and t-groups. It is suggested that the exercise be used only with groups which have established a high degree of personal contact.

Application Variables

    Thirty minutes. The exercise is 100 per cent non-verbal. The room must be large enough to allow members unrestrained movement.

Administrative Procedure

    a. The facilitator asks the members to stand up and form a circle.

    b. The facilitator then gives the following instructions: "I would like a volunteer to enter the middle of the circle. The member inside the large circle is to face one member at a time, get in touch with his feelings about the member he is facing, and let that person know non-verbally what he feels toward them."

    c. The facilitator should encourage members to make use of physical contact.

    d. After all members have been given an opportunity to enter the middle of the circle, the group members discuss the experience.

Suggestions for Facilitator Process

    Concentrate on the following during processing:

    a. *To members receiving feedback:* What feelings in yourself were you aware of when receiving feedback? Did you consis-

tently receive the same type of feedback? What was your
body doing as you received feedback?

b. *To members giving feedback:* How did you become aware of
what you were feeling toward the member you were facing?
Did you engage in much physical contact when giving feedback? What was your body doing when giving feedback? How
did you express yourself non-verbally?

Variations

None

HAND CONTACT

Subsidiary Goal(s)

a. To explore attitudes toward physical contact.
b. To explore attitudes toward closeness to authority.

Group Application

Twenty members or less. Applicable to any group, but most frequently used with encounter, personal growth, marathon and
t-groups.

Application Variables

Fifteen to thirty minutes. The exercise is 100 per cent non-
verbal.

Administrative Procedure

a. The facilitator asks the members to form a circle and hold
hands with the people on either side of them.
b. He says: "Close your eyes. Concentrate on the feelings you
are experiencing."
c. After two or three minutes he says: "Now concentrate on the
feelings and vibrations you are getting from your two hand
holding neighbors. Also, try to determine what feelings and
vibrations you are giving them."
d. After two or three minutes, the facilitator continues: "Continue to key in on your feelings. As you continue to do this I
will be going around the circle placing my hands on your

hands. Try to become aware of what feelings my touch arouses."

e. The facilitator then moves around the circle, clasping and squeezing each pair of clasped hands. He remains for a minute or two with each set of clasped hands.

f. When the facilitator has completed his hand clasping, the group discusses the experience.

Suggestions for Facilitator Process

Concentrate on the following during processing:

a. What reactions and feelings did you have when you first made hand contact? How did these reactions and feelings change as the exercise progressed? Why?

b. What were your reactions and feelings when I made contact? Did these feelings and reactions change? If yes, ask how and why.

c. What feelings and vibrations did you receive from your neighbors, from me, and from the group? What feelings were you trying to send?

d. What was your most negative feeling? Why? What was your most positive feeling? Why?

Variations

Variation I

a. Repeat step *a* through *e* of the original exercise.

b. Then say: "I will now take the place of anyone who wishes to do as I did. If you want to go around the circle and clasp the hands of the other members, silently step out and do so."

c. The option stated in step *b is* offered until all who wish to move around the circle have had the opportunity to do so.

d. During processing concentrate on the reasons for members' taking (or not taking) advantage of the step *b* option.

Intuition

INTUITION DEVELOPMENT #1

Subsidiary Goal(s)

a. To develop a sense of teamwork.

b. To observe member roles.

Group Application

Twenty members or less. Since teams are formed, the group size should be such that the members can be broken into teams of no less than three and no more than five. Applicable to any group.

Application Variables

Five to ten minutes. The exercise is 100 per cent non-verbal. The room must be large enough to comfortably accommodate the number of teams on hand. A tightly sealed box and any object chosen by the facilitator are needed for each team. One sheet of paper and one pencil are needed for each team.

Administrative Procedure

a. Prior to the start of the session, the facilitator prepares the boxes required. For example, with twenty members, four boxes would be needed for the four teams of five. The facilitator chooses any common object for enclosure in the boxes, e.g., book, jar, hairbrush, wallet, etc. For example, if a book is chosen, four books are used, one in each of the four boxes.

b. When the group session starts, the facilitator asks that the members *non-verbally* form teams. Specify the size of the teams as dictated by the large group size.

c. When the teams are formed, the facilitator has them sit on the floor in a circle. He then places one sealed box in the middle of each team's circle. He then says: "Without touching the box, use your intuition both individually and collectively to determine what common object is in the box before you."

d. After three minutes he says: "Write on your sheet of paper what you have intuited to be in the box."

e. After all teams have finished, he says: "Now, using any means you wish *except* opening the box, work as a team to intuit what is in the box. Do this non-verbally. When you have decided and agreed on what is in the box, write it down on your paper and return to the original large group circle."

f. When all teams are finished, the facilitator collects the papers, reads the intuitions, opens a box to reveal its contents and processes the exercise.

Suggestions for Facilitator Process

Concentrate on the following during processing:

a. How did you intuit your first choice? How did you work as a team? What roles did you observe?

b. How did you decide, as a team, what was in the box. What feelings were elicited by the exercise? How did you express these feelings? What non-verbal behavior did you observe in your team members?

c. To any who were right, how do you explain the fact that you were correct?

Variations

*Variation I

a. Instead of a box, place the objects in a large burlap bag. Tie it tightly so the object cannot be seen.

b. Then repeat steps c through f of the original exercise.

c. In processing, note that more teams will have intuited correctly. Ask if they believe it was intuition or if it was due to the fact that touch entered into the step e procedure.

INTUITION DEVELOPMENT #2

Subsidiary Goal(s)

a. To learn to coordinate the use of one's senses with one's intuitive abilities.

b. To learn to observe another's feeling as projected through his non-verbal body language.

c. To learn to give and receive feedback.

Group Application

Twelve members or less. Applicable to any group, but most frequently used with encounter, personal growth, marathon and t-groups. The exercise is particularly valuable when used with classroom or t-groups whenever sensory awareness and body language are the dynamics the facilitator wishes the members to concentrate on.

Application Variables

Twenty to twenty-five minutes or approximately two minutes per participant. The exercise is 100 per cent non-verbal. A cloth bag holding any uncommon or unusual object, paper and pencils for all participants, and one blindfold are needed. Examples of uncommon or unusual objects are; a pendant, a metal top of a coffee pot, a tomato, pear, apple, or head of lettuce, a plastic file box, etc.

Administrative Procedure

a. The facilitator asks for a volunteer to engage in an exercise designed to help the member learn to use his senses and his intuitive abilities.

b. The volunteer is told to sit in the middle of the group circle. He is then blindfolded.

c. The facilitator hands the volunteer the bag and says: "This bag contains an object. Using your senses of touch, taste, hearing and smelling along with your intuition, determine what is in the bag. When you believe you know what is in the bag, remove your blindfold, give me the bag, and write on your paper what you believe the object to be."

d. The facilitator tells the other members to observe the volunteer's non-verbal behavior and to be prepared to give him feedback later.

e. When the volunteer has finished, the exercise continues until all who wish to participate have had the opportunity to do so.

f. When all are done, the facilitator reveals the object, determines which members were right, and processes the experience.

Suggestions for Facilitator Process

Concentrate on the following during processing:

a. *To observers:* What non-verbal behaviors did you observe?

What feelings do you believe the volunteers were illustrating with these non-verbal behaviors?

b. *To the volunteers:* Are the observers correct? If not, what were you feeling?

c. *To all:* Why were those of you who were wrong unable to guess the object? How do those of you who were right explain your accuracy?

Variations

None

MATCHING INTUITION

Subsidiary Goal(s)

a. To learn the role projection plays in one's intuitive judgement making.

b. To learn how one copes with an extended period of non-verbal communication.

c. To learn to give and receive feedback.

d. To determine to what extent intuition differs between sexes.

Group Application

Twenty members or less. Since dyads are used, the group size must be even. Male-female dyads are recommended. Therefore, the group should be evenly composed of males and females. Applicable to any group, but most frequently used early in the life of encounter, personal growth, marathon and t-groups.

Application Variables

Forty to forty-five minutes. The exercise is 85 per cent non-verbal, with 15 per cent of the non-verbal activity being written, and 15 per cent verbal. Self-Assessment and Intuition forms and pencils are needed. Access to other rooms is advisable. If this is impossible, the room must be large enough to allow the dyads to feel some degree of privacy.

Administrative Procedure

a. The facilitator asks that the members complete the Self-Assessment form. This takes approximately five minutes.

b. He then asks that the members non-verbally form dyads with people they do not know well. If the composition of the groups is even by sexes, he may request that mixed dyads be formed.

c. He then says: "You will have twenty minutes to get to know each other. This is to be done non-verbally. Do not talk to each other. Using non-verbal means, try to learn as much as you can about who and what your partner is. You may stay here or go somewhere else. Remember, do not talk and be back here in twenty minutes."

d. After the dyads have returned, the facilitator gives each member an Intuition form and asks that it be completed. This takes approximately five minutes.

e. When all members are finished, he says: "You may now speak to each other. Compare your forms. Find out where you matched each other and investigate the reasons why. Find out where and why you failed to match each other. Discuss the experience."

f. After ten minutes, the facilitator has the group discuss the experience.

Suggestions for Facilitator Process

Concentrate on the following during processing:

a. *To dyads:* Share with us your matches and misses. Tell us why you think you were right or wrong. Did you guess frequently on the Intuition form? Why? How do those of you who did not guess frequently explain this phenomenon?

b. *To dyads:* What means of non-verbal communication did you use? Did any of you touch each other? Why? Why not? Do you feel you know each other better? If so, why? If not, why not?

c. *To all:* How did you feel as the dyadic communication started? How and why did your feelings change as the twenty minutes progressed? Who appeared to be the most intuitive, men or women? How do you explain this?

Variations

*Variation I

a. Whenever it becomes apparent that a member is having difficulty communicating with the group or is receiving a lot of feedback that he is "unknown" to the members, the facilitator has him complete the Self-Assessment form.

b. He then says: "We will take twenty minutes to get to know this individual. We will do it non-verbally. Do not talk to him or to each other. Use any means of non-verbal communication with him that you believe will help him to know you and you to know him."

c. After twenty minutes, the facilitator has each group member complete the Intuition form. The member communicated with does not complete it.

d. The facilitator has the member in question read his responses. As he does so, the other members tell him what they marked down. The reasons for similarities and differences are explored during this phase.

SELF-ASSESSMENT FORM

Complete the following items about you and your *typical* behavior. Use "yes" if you or your behavior is typically similar to the item under consideration. Use "no" if you or your behavior is typically opposite to the item under consideration.

Response

_____ 1. I am a happy person.

_____ 2. I am liberal in my behavior.

_____ 3. My dress and manners are important to me.

_____ 4. I enjoy touching people.

_____ 5. I enjoy being touched by people.

_____ 6. I like consistency in life and people more than I like change in life and people.

_____ 7. If I had a choice, I would prefer being with others to being with myself.

_____ 8. I am more extroverted than introverted.

_____ 9. I am anxious during prolonged silences.

_____10. I need to talk verbally with someone before I can feel I know them.

INTUITION FORM

Complete the following items about your dyadic partner and his *typical* behavior. Use "yes" if you intuitively feel he is similar to the item in question. Use "no" if you intuitively feel he is dissimilar to the item in question.

Response

_____ 1. He is a happy person.

_____ 2. He is liberal in his behavior.

_____ 3. His dress and manners are important to him.

_____ 4. He enjoys touching people.

_____ 5. He enjoys being touched by people.

_____ 6. He likes consistency in life and people more than he likes change in life and people.

_____ 7. If he had a choice, he would prefer being with others to being by himself.

_____ 8. He is more extroverted than introverted.

_____ 9. He is anxious during prolonged silences.

_____10. He needs to talk verbally with someone before he can feel he knows them.

Movement

*DANCE TO THE MUSIC

Subsidiary Goal(s)

a. To gain a greater awareness of one's body.

b. To provide an environment conducive to play.

c. To examine the dynamics involved in "letting go" of one's inhibitions.

d. To explore the process of fantasy.

Group Application

Twelve members or less. To be used only with encounter, personal growth, marathon and t-groups. Best results are obtained if the members have had some previous exposure to experiences centered on body movement.

Application Variables

Thirty to forty-five minutes. The exercise is 100 per cent non-verbal. A variety of records (four to seven) ranging from slow classical music to fast rock, as well as a phonograph, are required. The room must be large enough to allow members unrestrained movement. A room lighted only by candles will definitely add to the effect.

Administrative Procedure

a. The facilitator gives the following introduction: "Letting our body flow without control can be a beautiful and insightful experience. I have a number of musical records which represent various moods. I would like you to spread out. Remain standing and close your eyes."

b. When all are located, the facilitator continues: "Let your body begin to flow and express itself in any way you feel good with." He then plays the first selection. It is recommended that the selections begin with slow music and build up to fast or exciting music. The exercise is most effective if the music is entirely instrumental.

c. After the first selection, the facilitator states: "Now that we have begun to warm up, I am going to put a selection on with a faster pace and rhythm. Feel free to move about the room. Let your body and mind flow with the music."

d. The selections are played with no further verbal instructions. After the final selection, the members should be told to take a few minutes to absorb the experience fully. When they feel ready, the group rejoins for processing.

Suggestions for Facilitator Process

Concentrate on the following during processing:

a. What were you aware of during the experience? Did your moods change as the record selections changed? If so, how? Why? Were you able to let your body flow?

b. How did you feel while moving your body? Were you aware of your breathing? What have you learned about yourself?

Did you have any contact with other members? If not, why not?

Variations

Variation I

a. Have members pair off into dyads and dance together.
b. Follow the same basic procedure of sequential selections as used in the original exercise.

Variation II

a. Have the entire group dance *as* a group.
b. Follow the same basic procedure of sequential selections as used in the original exercise.

MOLDING AIR

Subsidiary Goal(s)

a. To explore the process of creativity.
b. To gain insight into the releasing of inhibitions.
c. To further one's insight into body awareness.

Group Application

Twelve members or less. To be used with encounter, personal growth, marathon and t-groups.

Application Variables

Fifteen to twenty minutes. The exercise is 100 per cent non-verbal. The room must be large enough to allow unrestricted movement. A darkened room illuminated by candle light will enhance the effect.

Administrative Procedure

a. The facilitator asks the members to spread out within the room and to close their eyes. The following instructions are then given: "Begin to move your arms through the air. Feel the air rush past your skin. Move your arms very slowly and very quickly. Get in touch with the different speeds at which you can comfortably move your arms."

b. After several minutes, the facilitator adds: "Begin to move the air around you with your arms. Begin to move the air in circles, squares and lines. Start shaping the air. Begin to mold it. Feel your arms touch the air. Feel the air's shape, weight, texture and temperature."

c. After the members appear to have begun to actually feel and shape the air, the facilitator states: "Start making sculptures from the air. Let your imagination run free. Create anything you wish. Make it as large or as small as you wish."

d. After several minutes, the facilitator says: "Open your eyes. Look at what you have created. Feel what you have created. After you feel you have truly gotten in touch with your creation, rejoin the circle for processing."

Suggestions for Facilitator Process

Concentrate on the following during processing:

a. What did you create? Why? What were you aware of while creating? Did your body begin to flow as the exercise progressed? If not, why not? If so, how do you explain this?

b. Was it difficult for you to get in touch with the air around you? If so, why? What did you see when you opened your eyes? What did you feel?

Variations

None

Perception

*HOW YOU ARE PERCEIVED

Subsidiary Goal(s)

a. To give and receive feedback.

b. To investigate how one copes with acceptance and rejection.

Group Application

Twelve members or less. To be used only with encounter, personal growth, marathon and t-groups. The exercise should be used after the group has met long enough for feelings of warmth, trust and care to have developed between the members.

Application Variables

Ten to fifteen minutes. The exercise is 100 per cent non-verbal. Each participant will need paper and pencil and a set of three by five cards. The set is comprised of three cards, one saying "positive," one "neutral," and the last "negative."

Administrative Procedure

a. The facilitator says: "In order to check our perception of others with their perceptions of themselves, we will engage in a non-verbal exercise."

b. He says: "Take your paper and pencil and write a response to the following question. How do you feel the other members of this group feel toward you?"

c. After all have finished, he says: "Answer the following. How do you feel the males in this group feel toward you?"

d. After all have finished, he says: "Answer this. How do you feel the females in this group feel toward you?"

e. The facilitator then says: "Take your set of cards. Write a capital M on the written side if you are a male and a capital F if you are a female.

Now, mill around non-verbally. Look at *every* member and gauge your feelings toward him."

f. After three to five minutes, the facilitator says: "Now give your cards away. Give them face down to the recipient. Give the positive card to the person you have the *most* positive feelings for, the negative to that person you have the *most* negative feelings for and the neutral card to the person you feel most neutral toward.

When all the cards have been given and received, return to your seats. Look at your cards. Then compare what you received with your written predictions.

g. After three to five minutes, he says: "Let's discuss this experience."

Suggestions for Facilitator Process

Concentrate on the following during processing:

a. How do you feel about the cards you received? Why do you

think you got them? How do they compare with your written predictions? Why do you think there is a disparity between cards received and predictions?

b. Did positive cards go more to the same or opposite sex? Why? Were the neutral and negative cards exchanged between same or opposite sexes? Why?

c. Tell us who you gave your cards to and why they received them? How did you feel about being forced to give away neutral and negative cards? Does anyone feel rejected? How are you coping with this feeling? What have you learned about yourself, others and the dynamics of perception?

Variations

None

LOOK ANY DIFFERENT?[1]

Subsidiary Goal(s)

a. To increase the member's awareness of his physical environment.

b. To experience frustration and anxiety.

Group Application

Twelve to twenty members. Applicable to any group. Best utilized with groups who have several tall members. This exercise is also quite effective when used with classroom groups *with* the students' parents participating.

Application Variables

Three minutes per volunteer. The exercise is 100 per cent nonverbal.

Administrative Procedure

a. The facilitator asks if any member, *particularly* tall ones, is willing to experience change in his perspectives of viewing his physical environment.

---

[1]Adapted from an exercise developed by Dan Millar, Coordinator of Interpersonal and Public Communication, Central Michigan University.

b. The group is told to cluster in a central area. The volunteer is told to go to the center of the cluster.

c. The facilitator tells the volunteer: "Kneel down. You are not to speak or to rise until I tell you to do so."
He then tells the rest of the members: "Mill around the volunteer. Talk to him and about him. Talk to each other. Do not, however, try to talk *with* the volunteer."

d. After three minutes, the volunteer is told to rise. Processing then occurs. After processing, another volunteer may be sought. The exercise is repeated until all who wish to experience it have had the opportunity.

Suggestions for Facilitator Process

Concentrate on the following during processing:

a. *To the volunteer:* What could you see? How did your visual perspectives differ from those you usually have in this group? How much impact did you have on the activity of the group? How do you feel about having been so unimportant? What affect did your new size have upon your perceptions of the group activity?

b. *To other members:* How did it feel to be so much bigger and more involved than the volunteer? Have your perceptions of him changed? If so, how and why?

Variations

None

ZOO

Subsidiary Goal(s)

a. To provide a structure conducive to creativity.
b. To allow members to act out their own fantasy.
c. To gain greater insight into the dynamics involved in play.

Group Application

Twelve members or less. To be used with encounter, personal growth, marathon and t-groups. Best results are obtained if the exercise is used after the group has had ample sessions to lessen inhibitions.

Application Variables

Thirty minutes. The exercise is 60 per cent non-verbal and 40 per cent verbal. The room must be large enough to allow members to move about unrestrained.

Administrative Procedure

a. The facilitator says: "Think of an animal which you feel most accurately represents you."

b. Each member is to tell the rest of the group the animal he has chosen and the rationale behind it.

c. After all members have assigned themselves animals, the members are told to spread out within the room. The facilitator then gives the following instructions: "When I say start, I would like all of you to become the animal that you have assigned yourself. Feel free to interact, play, explore and discover both by yourself and with the other animals. Start!"

d. After twenty minutes, the members discuss the experience.

Suggestions for Facilitator Process

Concentrate on the following during processing:

a. How did you feel when you became an animal? Were you surprised at some of the members' choices? If so, which members and why? What type of interactions occurred between yourself and other members?

b. What did you discover about yourself and other members? Was it difficult or easy for you to play? What type of physical contact did you engage in? Do you feel your role as an animal represented your role as a member in the group? If so, in what way?

Variations

None

Self-disclosure

*HERE'S HOW I SEE MYSELF

Subsidiary Goal(s)

a. To facilitate involvement of members encountering communication difficulties.

b. To ascertain a participant's self-concept as revealed through non-verbal communication of his body-concept.

c. To allow non-verbal feedback by other members as to their perceptions of your body-concept.

d. To provide the group with self-concept and body-concept data.

Group Application

Twelve members or less. To be used with encounter, personal growth, marathon, and t-groups whose members have developed warmth, care, and love for each other.

Application Variables

The authors have discovered that seldom will more than three members participate in this exercise during any one group session. Five to ten minutes per participant. The exercise is 100 per cent non-verbal. A carpeted room is needed.

Administrative Procedure

a. Whenever the facilitator notices that a member (or members) is having difficulty self-disclosing verbally, he asks him if he will participate in a non-verbal exercise designed to help him self-disclose.

b. The facilitator asks the member to lie on his back in the middle of the room. The other members form a circle around him, close enough to observe his actions, but far enough away to avoid encroaching on his private space. The group is told not to communicate in any way with the member.

c. The facilitator tells the member: "Try to relax. Close your eyes. Try to get into your body. Breath deeply and evenly." He continues in this manner until he feels the member is relaxed.

d. The facilitator then says: "Now, non-verbally, indicate those parts and areas of your body which you find displeasing."

e. When the member has finished, the facilitator requests that other members go to the member and non-verbally communicate to him which of his body parts and areas they find displeasing.

f. When step *e* has been completed, the facilitator tells the member to again relax. When he is relaxed, the facilitator says: "Non-verbally indicate those parts and areas of your body you find pleasing."

g. When the member has finished, the facilitator requests that other members go to the member and non-verbally communicate to him which of his body parts and areas they find pleasing.

h. Processing should occur at this point. After processing, other members who desire the experience should be given the opportunity to do so.

Suggestions for Facilitator Process

Concentrate on the following during processing:

a. *To the member:* How do you feel right now? What reactions do you have to the exercise? How do you now feel about your body? Which did you like most, having us communicate our pleasure or displeasure? Why? Which member's feedback was most meaningful? Why?

b. *To the observing members:* How do you explain the disparity of body-concept feedback? For example, some were pleased by hair, others displeased by it. How do you explain the similarity of body-concept feedback? For example, all were pleased by eyes.

c. *To all:* Why did some of you point at pleasing or displeasing body parts? Why did those of you who touched body parts do so? The authors have found that observers will seldom touch, or even point at, sexual body parts and areas. However, the volunteer frequently exhibits pleasure or displeasure with regard to sexual body parts and areas. These phenomena definitely warrant investigation by the facilitator and the group.

Variations

*Variation I

a. If a member exhibits too *negative* a self-concept, the facilitator may wish to have him engage *only* in the non-verbal communication of pleasing body parts and areas. This frequently helps the member become more positive in the way he sees himself.

*Variation II

a. If a member exhibits too *positive* a self-concept, the facilitator may wish to have him engage *only* in the non-verbal communication of displeasing body parts and areas. This frequently helps the member become aware that he is not perfect and does indeed have areas in which growth and improvement are required.

*PANDORA'S BOX

Subsidiary Goal(s)

a. To encounter the fantasy process.
b. To investigate the process of value clarification.

Group Application

Twelve members or less. To be used with encounter, personal growth, marathon and t-groups whose members have met long enough for feelings of warmth, care and trust to have developed.

Application Variables

Fifteen to twenty-five minutes. The exercise is 100 per cent non-verbal. The room must be large enough to allow the members to spread out without feeling unduly restricted.

Administrative Procedure

a. The facilitator says: "We are going to take the opportunity to non-verbally disclose our most cherished virtue and our most detested vice.
Please lie on the floor. Close your eyes and relax. Breathe evenly and deeply."
b. After a few minutes, he says: "Take a few minutes to reflect on your vices and virtues, your strengths and weaknesses.

Try to determine which virtue or strength you are most proud of. Determine which vice or weakness you are most ashamed of."

c. After two minutes, the facilitator says: "I have Pandora's Box in my hand. In it are all the vices and weaknesses, virtues and strengths of mankind.

I will open it. As the vices and virtues fly out and flood the room, I will identify them. I will call out as many of the vices and virtues as I can. When you hear me call a vice which you can most identify with, reach out and grab it. Also, reach out and grab the virtue you most identify with. The box is open."

d. He then reads of the following vices and virtues, strengths and weaknesses. He should use phrases such as: "Here comes the vice," "Here comes the virtue," "Here is the weakness," "Here is the strength," and similar phrases.

The following list is by no means exhaustive. We urge the facilitator to add to it.

Vices and Weaknesses		*Virtues and Strengths*	
1 adultery	19 greed	1 accepting	19 innocence
2 aggression	20 hate	2 beauty	20 just
3 anger	21 ignorant	3 brave	21 love
4 arrogance	22 immoral	4 care	22 loyal
5 callous	23 lax	5 charitable	23 meritorious
6 close-minded	24 lazy	6 chaste	24 moral
7 contempt	25 lying	7 concerned	25 obedient
8 corrupt	26 misbehavior	8 courage	26 open-minded
9 crime	27 offensive	9 courteous	27 prudent
10 cruel	28 perverse	10 creditable	28 respect
11 depravity	29 pride	11 empathic	29 secure
12 dishonest	30 selfish	12 ethical	30 self-control
13 envy	31 snobbish	13 faithful	31 sense of humor
14 evil	32 ungrateful	14 forgiving	32 sensitive
15 failure	33 unjust	15 friendly	33 temperate
16 fault-finding	34 unstable	16 graceful	34 understanding
17 force	35 vicious	17 honest	35 warm
18 gluttony	36 vindictive	18 hopeful	36 worthwhile

e. After reading the last vice and virtue, the facilitator says: "The box is empty. I know I missed some of the vices and virtues it contained and I am sorry. If you did not reach out and grab one of each, please use that which you chose at the beginning of this exercise.

Let's regroup and discuss what has just occurred."

Suggestions for Facilitator Process

Concentrate on the following during processing:

a. Tell us which vice or weakness you chose and why. Did you choose one and then later drop it and choose another? If so, why? If not, why not?

b. Tell us the virtue or strength you chose and why. Did you choose one and then later drop it and choose another? Why? Why not?

c. Who chose none, but instead used their own predetermined choices? Why? What have you learned about the other members? About yourself?

Variations

*Variation I

a. As a feedback exercise, have the vice and virtue list typed.

b. Have the members form dyads with each other based on closeness to the other person.

c. Give each person a list and say: "Peruse the list. Choose your greatest vice and virtue. Then choose the vice and virtue you feel is most evident in your partner. Signal each other when you are finished. Then verbally exchange your choices. Discuss your reasons as fully as possible."

*Variation II

a. Repeat Variation I *except,* during step *b,* have the dyads form based on distance to the other person.

*Variations III

a. For *positive* feedback, make a list of the strengths and virtues.

b. Have dyads formed based on closeness. Give the members the list and say: "Choose your three greatest virtues or strengths. Then, choose three which you feel are most appropriate for your partner. Signal each other when you are finished and then verbally share your choices."

*Variation IV

a. For *negative* feedback, make a list of the vices and weaknesses.

b. Have dyads formed based on distance. Give the members the list and say: "Choose your three greatest vices or weaknesses. Then, choose three which you feel are most appropriate for your partner. Signal each other when you are finished and then verbally share your choices."

*SELF COLLAGE[2]

Subsidiary Goal(s)

a. To obtain self-concept data.
b. To learn to communicate in symbolic, non-verbal forms.
c. To investigate the creative process.
d. To encourage participation.
e. To build deeper relationships.

Group Application

Group size is unlimited. If processing is to occur, the size should be twenty or less. Since dyads are used, group size should be even. Applicable to any group. Most frequently used during the early stages of the group's life.

Application Variables

Thirty minutes. The exercise is 80 per cent non-verbal and 20 per cent verbal. Paper shopping bags, scissors, glue or tape and a variety of magazines are needed. The room must be large enough to allow the members to spread out without feeling unduly restricted.

Administrative Procedure

a. The facilitator says: "We have been together long enough to have developed some insights into the "who" of each

---

[2]This exercise may also be used at the first group session to facilitate the *getting acquainted* process.

other. Today we are going to take the opportunity to non-verbally check out these perceptions. I have brought a number of magazines. You will also note that there are scissors, paper bags and tape (or glue).

When I tell you to start, you are to peruse the pile of magazines. Take any *one* which appeals to you. Then take one bag, one pair of scissors and a quantity of tape. You are then to find a comfortable spot in the room and create a collage which will tell us "who" you are. Try to avoid telling us the "what" of you. Are there any questions? . . . Please start."

b. After twenty minutes, the facilitator says: "Non-verbally form dyads with someone you don't feel you know too well. Then, take a few minutes to study the collage your partner created."

c. After two or four minutes, the facilitator says: "You have studied your partner's collage. Now, based on his collage, verbally tell him who you feel he is. Check with him concerning the accuracy of your interpretation of his collage."

d. When all dyads have finished discussing their interpretations, the members discuss the experience.

Suggestions for Facilitator Process

Concentrate on the following during processing:

a. Did you have difficulty describing the "who" of you? If so, why? How did you cope with this? Did you feel your collage told who you were?

b. *To the dyads:* Did your partner accurately interpret your collage? If not, why not? Did you use pictures, words and phrases or a combination of both? Do you know your partner better? Why? Why not? How do you feel about this experience? What have you learned about yourself? About your partner?

Variations

*Variation I

a. When used with groups whose members have developed rapport, warmth and insight between each other, the facil-

itator says: "We know each other quite well. Yet, our perceptions of others *do* differ from their perceptions of themselves. In order to check this out, we are going to make collages for ourselves and one other person.

You will have twenty minutes to make a collage for
yourself using the materials I brought. Tell us "who" you
are, not "what" you are. *Do not* show your finished collage
to anyone. Please start."

b. After twenty minutes, the facilitator says: "Form dyads with
the person you feel you know best."

c. When the dyads are formed, he continues: "Please go back
to your original spot. Make a collage for the "who" of your
partner. That is, be him and make the collage you feel he
has just made about who he is. You have twenty minutes."

d. After twenty minutes, the facilitator says: "Form the same
dyads. Exchange the collages. Look at them carefully. Then,
verbally discuss the similarities and differences between
your partner's collage and the collage you made for him."

e. During processing concentrate on the reasons for similarities
and differences between collages, new learnings which occurred, reactions to the feedback received and feelings about
the experience.

Self-expression

*BE THE MUSIC

Subsidiary Goal(s)

a. To provide an environment conducive to complete relaxation.

b. To gain greater awareness of the differences between thinking and feeling.

Group Application

Twelve members or less. To be used with encounter, personal
growth, marathon and t-groups. Best results are obtained if the
exercise is used after the group has experienced an intense
emotional experience.

Application Variables

Thirty minutes to one hour. The exercise is 100 per cent non-verbal. A stereo system of good reproductive quality and a diverse selection of records are required. The room should be large enough to allow members to spread out.

Administrative Procedure

a. The facilitator asks the group to reach a consensus as to the types of music to be played.
b. He then asks the members to spread out and to lie down with their eyes closed.
c. The facilitator tells the members he will play the selections that the group has reached a consensus on. The selections will be played at a very high volume. Members are told to keep their eyes closed and do absolutely nothing. They are asked *not* to think or feel, but rather to totally let go of themselves and become part of the music. (The effect is enhanced by a darkened room lit only by one candle.)
d. After the selection or selections are finished, the members are given some time to absorb the experience. Processing then occurs.

Suggestions for Facilitator Process

Concentrate on the following during processing:
a. Were you able to let go of yourself? Why? Why not? What did the experience mean to you? Did you achieve complete relaxation?
b. What insights did you gain about yourself? Did you become part of the music?

Variations

None

MUSIC DICTATES ART

Subsidiary Goal(s)

a. To learn to express, through art, one's feelings and moods.
b. To learn to overcome inhibitions.

Group Application

Twenty members or less. Applicable to any group, but most frequently used with encounter, personal growth, marathon and t-groups.

Application Variables

Thirty minutes. The exercise is 100 per cent non-verbal. A variety of drawing materials are needed. There should be a sufficient number of sketch pads, brushes, paint, charcoal, and other art materials to insure that all members will be able to draw *simultaneously* if they so desire. A tape or cassette recorder is also needed.

Administrative Procedure

a. Prior to the session, the facilitator records on tape two and three minute selections from a variety of musical sources. A typical tape would include selections from rock, acid rock, country and western, orchestral, pop, operatic, classical and other forms of music.

b. At the start of the session, the facilitator says: "Let's take the opportunity to learn to overcome some of our inhibitions and to learn to express ourselves spontaneously.

I have recorded a variety of music. When I turn it on, I want you to let the music come into your being. Absorb it. Feel it. Let it move you.

When you experience a mood or when you sense the presence in yourself of unexpressed feelings, get up, take some art materials and draw. Try to take the feelings that are within your being and put them into your drawing. Let your art work express your mood and feelings.

If you wish to draw in teams, do so. If a member is drawing and you want to complete his work for him, ask him, nonverbally, if you can do so.

Feel free to experiment. Do not, however, talk to another member."

c. The facilitator places the art materials on the floor and turns on the recording. He may wish to illustrate by expressing himself or he may wish to wait until others have done so. If he notices non-verbal cues being emitted that the music is affecting an individual who is not expressing himself, he may ask that member to "get up, take some art material, and express what is going on in you."

d. After thirty minutes, the group discusses the experience.

Suggestions for Facilitator Process

Concentrate on the following during processing:

a. What feelings and moods were you experiencing? Which music elicited them? Why? How did your art work express these feelings?

b. Whose art work was most expressive? Why do you say this? Whose art work was most spontaneous? Why do you say this? Why did some of you draw so seldom?

c. What occurred to make you decide to work in teams? How did you feel when someone asked to help you? Was this experience worthwhile and meaningful for you? If yes, why? If no, why not?

Variations

None

MUSICAL EXPRESSION

Subsidiary Goal(s)

a. To learn to become spontaneous in non-verbally expressing feelings and moods.

Group Application

Twelve members or less. To be used with encounter, personal growth, marathon and t-groups whose members have developed feelings of warmth and acceptance for each other.

Application Variables

Thirty minutes. The exercise is 100 per cent non-verbal. A tape or cassette recorder is needed.

Administrative Procedure

    a. Prior to the session, the facilitator records on tape two and three minutes selections from a *variety* of musical sources. A typical tape would include selections from rock, acid rock, country and western, orchestral, pop, operatic, classical and other forms of music.

    b. When the session starts, the facilitator says: "Let's take the opportunity to learn to overcome some of our inhibitions and to learn to express ourselves spontaneously.

    I have recorded a variety of music. When I turn it on, I want you to let the music come into your being. Absorb it. Feel it. Let it move you.

    When you experience a mood or when you sense the presence in yourself of unexpressed feelings, get up and express your feelings and mood.

    You can dance, hum, move about expressing your emotions, concentrate on hand or body expressions, and so forth. Do not, however, make physical or verbal contact with other members.

    You will probably feel silly, be embarrassed, be unsure of "how to do it," and so on. *Don't* give into these feelings. Get up and conquer them by spontaneously expressing your feelings and mood."

    c. The facilitator starts the recording. He may wish to illustrate by expressing himself or he may wish to wait until others have done so. If he notices non-verbal cues being emitted that the music is affecting an individual who is not expressing himself, he may ask that member to "get up and express what is going on in you."

    d. After thirty minutes, the group discusses the experience.

Suggestions for Facilitator Process

    Concentrate on the following during processing:

    a. What feelings and moods were you experiencing? Which music elicited them? Why? How did you express these feelings?

b. Who was most expressive? Why do you say this? Who was most spontaneous? Why do you say this? Why did some of you participate so seldom?
c. How do you now feel? Was this experience worthwhile and meaningful for you? If yes, why? If no, why not?

Variations

None

INDEX